Advance praise for *Signed, Sealed, Delivered*

This book offers an incredible abundance of wisdom and reflection on the theologies of the rites of initiation of the Episcopal Church, and fills a long-standing gap in our literature on confirmation. Written by some of our deepest and most innovative liturgists, theologians, and educators today, *Signed, Sealed, Delivered* stands as the most important work on its subject to date. This book is recommended for all who care about the ministry of all the baptized and the life of the church.

—*The Rev. Dr. Sheryl A. Kujawa-Holbrook,*
Claremont School of Theology, Bloy House

The precise meaning and intention of confirmation, as well as its relationship to the primary sacrament of Baptism continues to puzzle many in the Episcopal Church. Sharon Ely Pearson has compiled an excellent book that offers her own keen insights on the topic, as well as thoughtful essays from a knowledgeable group of others. *Signed, Sealed, Delivered* resists offering on*e simple* solution to the puzzle, but intends to promote an exciting and deeper conversation across the Church, encouraging us all to consider Confirmation, Baptism, and the overriding question of Christian formation and mature faith in richer, deeper and more significant ways for the sake of Christ and Christ's Church. I welcome and endorse this resource and intend to use it to generate meaningful conversation and practices in my own diocese.

—*The Rt. Rev. William H. (Chip) Stokes, Bishop of New Jersey*

Signed, Sealed, Delivered begins with a complete history of confirmation that has long been needed in the church. It continues with views from diverse Christian formation leaders and best practices that will help any current confirmation program. This should be on the shelf of every person in the church who is connected with confirmation programs.

—*Randall Curtis, Ministry Developer for Youth and Young Adults,*
Episcopal Diocese of Arkansas and President of Forma

At last this much-needed resource not only untangles the muddled history of confirmation, it points in useful, practical ways to a theology that befits a Church that is truly concerned with the formation of children, youth, and adults.

—*Dr. Fredrica Harris Thompsett, Mary Wolfe Professor Emerita*
of Historical Theology, Episcopal Divinity School

This is a useful, wise, and hopeful book about a highly contested and complex topic. Bringing together accurate historical and canonical summaries, insightful pastoral wisdom, personal stories, and examples of good practices from a variety of contexts, *Signed, Sealed, Delivered* will help clergy and Christian educators navigate the choppy waters that swirl around confirmation and emerge with clearer theology and—infinitely more important—a conviction of the spiritual value of a renewed and enriched rite.

—*The Rev. Dr. Susanna Singer, Associate Professor of Ministry Development, and*
Director, Doctor of Ministry Program, Church Divinity School of the Pacific

This useful book offers thoughtful, provocative essays that should stimulate a deeper conversation in the church about the rite of Confirmation and appropriate preparation for it. It is important reading for anyone interested in confirmation.

—*The Rev. Canon James F. Turrell, Ph.D., Associate Dean for Academic Affairs and Mills Professor of Divinity, School of Theology, University of the South*

This book is a "must read" for clergy and Christian Educators who prepare persons for confirmation. With clarity and insight, Sharon Ely Pearson and the other experienced contributors present a variety of thoughtful approaches to the theology of confirmation as well as practical suggestions to make the Confirmation process as meaningful as possible.

—*Thomas G. O'Brien III, Vice-Chair of the Standing Commission on Lifelong Christian Formation and Education & a Lay Deputy to General Convention from the Diocese of Southeast Florida (2006–present)*

What a gift Sharon Ely Pearson and her co-authors have created! History, ecclesiology, theology, pedagogy, and practical how-to's all contribute to a tapestry woven on the loom of tradition, to focus God's people on intentionally claiming their baptismal calling. This book provides an invitation to engage questions of faith and formation, both as an individual and in community.

—*Demi Prentiss, Certified Ministry Developer, Episcopal Diocese of Fort Worth*

For any parent, leader, or member of the church who wrestles with when someone should be confirmed, Sharon Ely Pearson's book *Signed, Sealed, Delivered* will help you think through the meaning of your own confirmation while providing a history of the rite and possibilities for its future.

—*The Rt. Rev. W. Andrew Waldo, VIIIth Bishop of the Episcopal Diocese of Upper South Carolina*

Youth Ministers across the church cry out for the best, the most useful, the latest, most creative, and sometimes the easiest confirmation resources all the time. Too often we are looking for a simple and prescribed fix to fulfill an articulated expectation of parish, clergy, and/or bishop for confirmation preparation for our teens, when we don't really have a thorough or common understanding of confirmation ourselves. This book brings depth, history, thoughtfulness, truth-telling, creativity, and hope to this persistent sacrament that we can't seem to fully grasp or agree upon.

—*Bronwyn Clark Skov, Missioner for Youth Ministries for The Episcopal Church*

Confirmation is a subject the Church has had difficulty talking about because we lack a vocabulary. These essays are informative, insightful, and imaginative. They enable the Church to have a wide and deep conversation about this rite for this complex and diverse time.

—*The Rt. Rev. Porter Taylor, Episcopal Diocese of Western North Carolina*

Signed, *Sealed,* DELIVERED

THEOLOGIES OF CONFIRMATION FOR THE 21ST CENTURY

Compiled by Sharon Ely Pearson

Morehouse Publishing
NEW YORK · HARRISBURG · DENVER

Unless otherwise noted, the Scripture quotations contained herein are from the New Revised Standard Version Bible, copyright © 1989 by the Division of Christian Education of the National Council of Churches of Christ in the U.S.A. Used by permission. All rights reserved.

Morehouse Publishing, 4785 Linglestown Road, Suite 101, Harrisburg, PA 17112

Morehouse Publishing, 19 East 34th Street, New York, NY 10016

Morehouse Publishing is an imprint of Church Publishing Incorporated.
www.churchpublishing.org

Cover design by Laurie Klein Westhafer
Typeset by Rose Design

Library of Congress Cataloging-in-Publication Data

Signed, sealed, delivered : theologies of confirmation for the 21st century / compiled by Sharon Ely Pearson.
    pages cm
Includes bibliographical references.
 ISBN 978-0-8192-2891-8 (pbk.)—ISBN 978-0-8192-2892-5 (ebook) 1. Confirmation—Episcopal Church. 2. Episcopal Church—Membership. 3. Confirmation—Anglican Communion. 4. Anglican Communion—Membership. I. Pearson, Sharon Ely, editor of compilation.
 BX5949.C7S54 2014
 264'.03082—dc23
                          2013048413

Printed in the United States of America

Contents

PART IV / A THEOLOGY OF CONFIRMATION FOR THE FUTURE

Introduction

Today in the Anglican tradition, the term "confirmation" carries a dual meaning. For some, it is the sacramental, post-baptismal rite of blessing in which initiation is sealed by the Spirit. For others, it is the time for public ratification of one's baptismal promises. In terms of adolescent participation, confirmation is often viewed as a rite of passage, a puberty rite that provides strengthening of gifts of the Spirit, as one becomes an adult in the faith community. For many, it is a combination of all three meanings. Orthodox theologian Alexander Schmemann writes, "No other liturgical act of the Church has provoked more theological controversies than this second sacrament of initiation; none has received a greater variety of interpretations."[1]

"Equipping the Baptized for Ministry in the Episcopal Church" was the umbrella theme for four resolutions (A041, A042, A043, A044)[2] brought to the 77th General Convention in 2012 from the Standing Commission on Lifelong Christian Formation and Education. Focused on bringing the *Constitution and Canons of the Episcopal Church* into conformity with the baptismal theology of the Book of Common Prayer (1979), which teaches that "Holy Baptism is full initiation by water and the Holy Spirit into Christ's Body the Church" (BCP p. 299), these resolutions immediately became known as the "confirmation resolutions," receiving passionate testimony from those "pro" and those "con" during the Education Committee hearings on this group of resolutions.

Many who spoke against these resolutions felt it would mean removing the rite of Confirmation from our churches. Those who spoke in favor of the resolutions were articulate about the Episcopal Church's understanding of baptism as full membership in the Church. In committee, deputies were

---

1. Gerard Austin, *Anointing with the Spirit—The Rite of Confirmation: The Use of Oil and Chrism* (New York: Pueblo Publishing Company, 1985), ix.

2. Resolution A041 Amend Canon I.17 was regarding the training of leadership in history and polity of the Episcopal Church. Resolution A042 Amend Canons I.1.1(b), Canon I.1.2(a), Canon I.25, Canon I.4.1(c), Canon I.4.3(d), Canon I.9.7, Canon III.4.1, Canon IV.17.3; Resolution A043 Amend Constitution Article I, Section 4; and Resolution A044 Review Confirmation Requirements in Title III each involved striking the word "confirmation" as prerequisite to holding an appointed or elected office at all levels the church's governance.

much more open to making changes in the canons, while bishops were not. A042, A043, and A044 were sent back for further study to the Standing Commission on Ministry Development. A041 was rejected.

This scenario is not new to General Convention, diocesan conversations, or the House of Bishops. At the 73rd General Convention of the Episcopal Church in July 2000, Resolution A103 called upon the Standing Commission on Ministry Development to explore the *Canons of the Episcopal Church* regarding confirmation and the requirement for a member of the Episcopal Church to be confirmed in order to be licensed in any of various ministries, vote as an elector in congregational meetings, or to be considered a "full" member of the Episcopal Church. The subsequent report issued in January 2003 stated that the argument of confirmation being a "sacrament looking for a theology, is moot."[3] Despite the report, many questions were not answered, continuing the disagreement of the age of when one should be confirmed, it's timing in the process of initiation, and the preparation required.

Resolution B013, passed by the 76th General Convention in 2009, urged the Standing Commission on Lifelong Christian Formation and Education to collaborate with the Baptismal Consultation of the Associated Parishes for Liturgy and Mission to "provide to the next General Convention educational resources for formation in Episcopal identity and rites to celebrate that identity, educational resources for training the baptized for leadership positions in the Church and rites for entering leadership positions, and any proposed revisions to the canons to conform them to the baptismal theology of the Book of Common Prayer." Since first being convened by the Presiding Bishop in 2007, the work of the Baptismal Consultation has been to bring the Episcopal Church canons in line with the baptismal theology of the Book of Common Prayer. The greatest variance between the canons and the prayer book's baptismal theology lies in the occasional requirement of confirmation to hold office in the Episcopal Church. That's what brought out the passion for several mornings at 7:00 a.m. in July 2012 in Indianapolis.

The conversation about the role of confirmation in the life of our Church is not going away. Since July 2012, numerous editorials and articles

---

3. Office of Ministry Development, "The Future of Confirmation for the Episcopal Church in the 21st Century," General Convention 2003 Blue Book Documents.

have been written exploring how confirmation might play a role in a twenty-first century church, especially in light of the decline of members and the increase of adults (with their families) coming to the Episcopal Church from the Roman Catholic tradition and Latino communities. The practice of preparation for Confirmation differs widely across the Church within and between dioceses, and the preparation used for leaders (such as Vestry) into the history, doctrine, and polity of the Episcopal Church is just as nebulous.

Despite the 2012 resolutions not passing (being rejected in Committee), they were discussed in both the House of Bishops and House of Deputies, allowing for the first of what will hopefully continue to be many conversations about what role confirmation plays in the life of our Church.

This book seeks to help continue that conversation. It has been my desire to gather the historical perspectives of confirmation together in one place alongside the practical and faith formation needs of youth and adults in our congregations since I first began serious study in the history and theology of confirmation in 2000 while working on my thesis for Virginia Theological Seminary. That led to new guidelines adopted in the Diocese of Connecticut in 2005 and a variety of speaking engagements in other dioceses struggling to develop their own strategies, including the writing of their own curriculum and customaries. Most of these conversations focused on the preparation of youth for confirmation, as well as what the meaning of a "mature decision" meant.

Congregations across our Church continue to encourage adolescents to seek confirmation. Some of this may be due to parental expectation, with the concern that if their children are not confirmed they will "leave the church" or at least, "we should confirm them before they go." But in many cases it is the young people themselves who wish to take this step. The Church's understanding and articulation of confirmation can help inform how our young people will continue on their faith journey and become active, participating members of our congregations, as well as how the Church supports them.

Almost fifteen years later, conversation is still needed; opinions are passionate and emotions run high. By collecting relevant information in one place, along with a process for congregations and dioceses to have deep conversations about the meaning and role of confirmation, I hope this book will open up new ways for all our members—church leaders (lay and ordained), parents, and young people—to have such an authentic dialogue.

I am grateful to the many individuals who accepted my invitation to share their perspective on the theology, meaning, practicalities, and role of confirmation in our Church today. Many of them were present at those early morning hearings before the Education Committee in Indianapolis. I give thanks that our Church has such passionate voices in caring for how we affirm our faith and live out our baptismal promises in the world.

Sharon Ely Pearson
1st Sunday of Advent, 2013
Norwalk, Connecticut

PART I

CHRISTIAN INITIATION

I therefore, the prisoner in the Lord, beg you to lead a life worthy of the calling to which you have been called, with all humility and gentleness, with patience, bearing with one another in love, making every effort to maintain the unity of the Spirit in the bond of peace. There is one body and one Spirit, just as you were called to the one hope of your calling, one Lord, one faith, one baptism, one God and Father of all, who is above all and through all and in all.

—Ephesians 4:1–6

CHAPTER 1

Rites of Initiation
in the Christian Tradition

Christian baptism in the New Testament is a complete and adequate entrance into a new relationship with the Father, the Messiah and the Holy Spirit, becoming a full member of the new Church. Households were baptized together, including slaves and children. If children could not answer the questions of renunciation and commitment for themselves, others answered for them.[1] The newly baptized emerged from the water and (in many parts of the Church) were anointed, usually over the entire body. Being marked with the sign of the cross with oil, a part of the rite called consignation, the newly baptized were then re-clothed (later in the era they received white garments). Being brought into the Eucharistic assembly for the first time, they shared in the kiss of peace and the people's prayers, made their own offering of bread and wine, and received the Body and Blood of Christ. Baptism was seen as a water moment of the washing from sin and a cleansing act of forgiveness. The anointing, a representation of the rich, flowing life of the Spirit,[2] was a sealing of the gift of the Holy Spirit, being marked as Christ's own forever. The name "Christian" means anointed.[3] The use of anointing in making prophets, priests, and kings would carry a spiritual association to any Jew, including the first Christians.

There are many allusions to anointing, such as in 2 Cor 1:21–22, that speak of receiving the seal of the Holy Spirit as a sign of commissioning

---

1. Daniel B. Stevick, *Baptismal Moments: Baptismal Meanings* (New York: The Church Hymnal Corporation, 1987), 9.

2. Charles P. Price, "Appendix—Occasional Paper Number Four—Rites of Initiation," *Baptism & Ministry: Liturgical Studies 1* (New York: The Church Hymnal Corporation, 1994), 96.

3. Donald J. Parsons, "Some Theological and Pastoral Implications of Confirmation," in Kendig Brubaker Cully, ed., *Confirmation Re-Examined* (Harrisburg, PA: Morehouse Publishing, 1982), 55.

for apostolic ministry. In the King James Version of the Bible, the Greek word translated as "commissioned" means literally "anointed."[4] The conveying of responsibility by the laying on of hands was also an ancient practice existing in Israel; it was a regular and agreed upon method of either transferring or shifting responsibility in the community. This custom predates Exodus, and following this laying on of hands, or public binding, a participation in a common meal as a form of communion with the divine ancestor was shared. Many of these Jewish customs found their way into the initiation rites of the early Church.

While the water ritual was the central part of baptism and was seen as the act of initiation, the laying on of hands, the "stirring up" of the Spirit, had an eschatological quality.[5] In Acts 8:4–8, 14–17, the mission of Peter and John to Samaria laid hands on those who had previously been baptized, and they received the Holy Spirit. Daniel Stevick believes this narrative is about a missionary advance into schismatic Jewish Samaria and should not be seen as a continuation of the initiation rite.[6] In Acts 19:1–7, twelve disciples in Ephesus had been baptized with John the Baptizer's "baptism of repentance," but had not received (nor heard of) the Holy Spirit. They are then baptized "in the name of the Lord Jesus" by Paul, and then through the laying on of Paul's hands, receive the Holy Spirit. These stories from Acts of the Apostles have led to many interpretations of how the Spirit is received throughout Church history.

The writings of the Apostolic Fathers speak of water as Spirit-giving. Clement of Rome (c. 90) is aware that we have "one God and one Christ and one Spirit of Grace who was poured out on us." *The Epistle of Barnabas* (c. 90s) opens by asking its readers to share how the Spirit is "poured out on them from the riches of the Lord's fount."[7] In the *Shepherd of Hermas* (c. 140–150), there are six examples of where the readers are said to have received the Spirit, in most cases with water.

At this time, converts to Christianity were now being made almost exclusively from the ranks of pagans, so a period of preparation for

---

4. Charles P. Price and Louis Weil, *Liturgy for Living*, revised ed. (New York: The Seabury Press, 1979), 79.

5. Edward N. West, "The Rites of Christian Initiation in the Early Church," in Kendig Brubaker Cully, ed., *Confirmation: History, Doctrine and Practice* (Greenwich, CT: The Seabury Press, 1962), 9.

6. Stevick, *Baptismal Moments*, 6.

7. J. D. C. Fisher, "Confirmation: Then and Now," *Alcuin Club*, no. 60 (London: S.P.C.K., 1978), 3.

baptism became an important rule. The immediate and personal responsibility for the spread of the Christian mission that characterized the apostolic age was not as important as renouncing Satan and confessing the faith of Christ. There was a period of catechesis in which the story of Jesus Christ was shared, as well as the teachings of the apostles and prayers of the people. This preparation took place over a period of time prior to the celebration of Easter when all new converts were baptized into the Church. The earlier "confirmation" to mission of the Gospel was no longer as immediate as it had been during the apostolic period. Following their baptism, the new Christians were welcomed into the household of faith and participated in the community meal, the Eucharist.

As the early church grew and spread, there were differences in the rite of initiation as practiced in Carthage and in Rome. The first documented description of baptism in the Church is from Tertullian (c. 155–220) of Carthage, describing the washing as cleansing and blessing of our bodies so that the imposition of hands can invite the coming of the Holy Spirit. He speaks of the Spirit's resting on the waters of baptism, being active throughout the rite.[8] In Tertullian's *Liber de Baptismo*, he says, "the giving of Baptism is the right of the High Priest, who is the bishop and others have it only as delegates."[9] For him, it is not the water but the "seal" which imparts the Spirit, being given by the bishop. The whole rite remains one service, and its "minister" is the bishop. Noted liturgist Dom Gregory Dix asserts that this is the general pre-Nicene understanding of the rite of Baptism.

The first known text of a full baptismal liturgy can be found in the *Apostolic Tradition* (c. 215) of Hippolytus (c. 170–236), from the church in Rome.[10] It is elaborate: thanksgiving over oil of thanksgiving, exorcism of oil of exorcism, renunciation of Satan, anointing with oil of exorcism by a presbyter, affirmation of a creed, baptism in water, anointing with oil of thanksgiving by a presbyter. Following their baptism, drying themselves and being newly vested, the neophytes are brought into the church. At the end of the rite according to *Apostolic Tradition 21–22*, the bishop laid a

---

8. Parsons, in *Confirmation Re-Examined*, 48.

9. Timothy J. Turner, "Welcoming the Baptized: Anglican Hospitality with the Ecumenical Enterprise," *Joint Liturgical Studies 34*—The Alcuin Club and Group for Renewal of Worship (Cambridge, England: Grove Books Ltd., 1996), 14.

10. Price, *Baptism & Ministry*, 88.

hand on each of the candidates, in prayer.[11] Although the rite of Hippolytus appears to presuppose that most of the candidates would be mature persons who had gone through extensive preparation, there is also a rubric regarding who these neophytes might be:

> They shall baptize the little children first. And if they can answer for themselves, let them answer. But if they cannot, let the parents answer or someone from their family.[12]

Thus we have sponsors speaking on behalf of children who were too young to speak for themselves. Infant candidates are baptized, confirmed, and communicated at one sacramental action with the bishop present, just as adult candidates are initiated into the Christian community.

Theologian Aidan Kavanagh does not believe that the bishop's "confirmation prayer" is an *epiclesis* of the Holy Spirit, but a dismissal, or *missa*, leading to the breaking of the bread and admission to the Eucharistic community.[13] He believes that the structure we know as "confirmation" today originated with this liturgical action. The purpose of a *missa* rite was to conclude and formally "seal" a unit of public worship or instruction by dismissing the assembly with prayer and physical contact by its chief minister—bishop or presbyter.

Cyprian (c. 200–258), Bishop of Carthage, believed in the presence and power of the Spirit in Baptism, but the Spirit was given and received by the power of the laying on of hands.[14] Ambrose of Milan (340–397) speaks of a "spiritual seal" and a "perfecting" or invocation of the Holy Spirit and its gifts on the neophytes, which takes place after the post-baptismal anointing and foot washing.[15] With Ambrose, it appears that this northern Italian practice began the Western theory that confirmation is the "completion" of baptism.[16]

---

11. Paul Turner, *Source of Confirmation: From the Fathers through the Reformation* (Collegeville, MN: The Liturgical Press, 1993), 12–13.

12. Fisher, "Confirmation: Then and Now," 137.

13. Aidan Kavanagh, *Confirmation: Origins and Reform* (New York: Pueblo Publishing Company, Inc., 1988), ix–x.

14. Allen F. Bray, III, "Baptism and Confirmation: A Relationship of Process," in Cully, ed., *Confirmation Re-Examined*, 49.

15. Kavanagh, *Confirmation*, 53.

16. West, in Cully, ed., *Confirmation: History, Doctrine and Practice*, 10.

During the fourth century, the Church increased in numbers and many of its members lived in remote rural areas. The presence of a bishop was not always possible, as baptisms were a more frequent occurrence in an expanding church. Jerome (c. 347–420) writes of his distress that presbyters and deacons in churches that are far from the bigger cities have baptized many without the bishop's presence.[17]

As the Church expanded, practices adapted and changed to the local circumstances. John Chrysostom (347–407) describes the rites of Antioch as having no anointing following baptism; it is in the water that the Holy Spirit descends on the baptized "through the words and hands of the priest."[18] In different regions of the Church, the newly baptized received a signing with the cross (Milan, Rome, Spain, and North Africa), a laying on of hands (Rome and North Africa), a second anointing by the bishop (Rome), and even in some places *pedilavium*, or foot washing (Milan and Spain).[19]

During Augustine's time (354–430), people were largely illiterate, so Christian preparation took place through worship, biblical preaching, and reading Scripture aloud. Catechumens continued to go through a lengthy period of instruction in the faith. Augustine's doctrine that baptism cleansed inherited sin and guilt reinforced the practice of baptizing children as early as possible. Pope Innocent I also stated that children were to receive the sacrament upon their baptism, and he decreed that consignation of baptized infants should be only by the bishop, for this specific ministry belongs only to those of "the highest rank of the pontificate."[20] The hand laying and bishop's participation were viewed as a pastoral presence, not to be seen as a completion of the full initiation rite of the water baptism.

Local councils (Riez in 439 and Orange in 441) are when the words *confirmare* or *perficere* are used in reference to particular rites associated with the ministry of bishops in baptismal initiation.[21] These rites involved the imposition of hands with prayer for the Holy Spirit. Innocent I

---

17. Fisher, "Confirmation: Then and Now," 127.
18. Stevick, *Baptismal Moments*, 9.
19. Maxwell E. Johnson, *The Rites of Christian Initation: Their Evolution and Interpretations.* (Collegeville, MN: The Liturgical Press, 1999),157; Stevick, *Baptismal Moments*, 9.
20. Stevick, *Baptismal Moments*, 15.
21. Johnson, 142.

reinterpreted the *missa* as to be a ceremonial gesture of signation on the forehead of the neophytes.[22] Outside of southeast Gaul, the word confirmation is not used in regard to the post-baptismal rites, but of Eucharistic communion. The chalice "completes" the eating of the consecrated bread, or, as with Alcuin, the bread and cup "confirms" the participants.[23]

A Pentecost sermon attributed to the semi-Pelagian bishop Faustus of Riez (southern Gaul) around 450 serves as a benchmark for the classic Western theology of confirmation.

> In baptism we are washed; after baptism we are strengthened. And although the benefits of rebirth suffice immediately for those about to die, nevertheless the helps of confirmation are necessary for those who will prevail. Rebirth in itself immediately saves those needing to be received in the peace of this blessed age. Confirmation arms and supplies those needing to be preserved for the struggles and battles of this world.[24]

Faustus also argued that confirmation should be deferred until a suitable maturity had been attained. Prior to this homily, Hispano-Gallican liturgies were simple baptisms in water followed by a single chrismation by a presbyter or deacon.[25] From the sixth through the ninth centuries, the Romanizing and sacramentalizing of Hispano-Gallican practices of episcopal disciplinary oversight of baptism became known as "confirmation of neophytes."[26]

Eighth century reforms under Charlemagne sought a greater standardization of liturgical, ecclesiastical, and political practice in the West. Service books were obtained from Rome, and new texts were introduced throughout Europe. Episcopal confirmation was part of the Roman rites, so became part of the liturgy in places that had not known it before.[27] This was reinforced by Rabanus Maurus (d. 835), Bishop of Mainz who speculated on the theological significance of the separation of the two rites, stating that "episcopal chrismation and laying on of hands brings

---

22. Kavanagh, *Confirmation*, 69.

23. Frank C. Quinn, "Confirmation Reconsidered: Rite and Meaning" *Worship 59* (July 1985), 362.

24. Johnson, 146.

25. Kavanagh, *Confirmation*, 66-67.

26. Kavanagh, *Confirmation*, 69.

27. Stevick, *Baptismal Moments*, 16.

the grace of the Spirit into the Baptized with all the fullness of sanctity, power and knowledge."[28] His rite also contained a rite of confirmation to be celebrated at a later time. The length of time between the two parts of initiation (baptism and confirmation) grew longer.

In the middle of the ninth century, Pseudo-Isidore, compiler of the *False Decretals*, took parts of Faustus' sermon and attributed them to Melchiades and Urban I, popes who lived (and died) during church persecutions in the early fourth century.[29] From the eighth to the twelfth centuries, the rite of initiation consisted of baptism, confirmation, and first communion being three parts of one whole, not always experienced at the same moment, with each additional rite adding new strength to the individual.

In the eleventh century a major change in the practice of the doctrine of "real presence" began to influence the life of the Church. In many areas of the Church, infants ceased to receive communion, believing the grace that they received at baptism could suffice until they were of an age to commit actual sin. They could not receive the presence of Christ until they were thought to understand its meaning, and the age of seven became a standard in many regions. This "age of discretion" has shaped Western thinking ever since.

The Middle Ages were a time when each action comprising the rites of initiation took on a separate meaning, to include: the work of the Holy Spirit, the timing of each event, the catechumenal period, and the administrator of such actions. Thomas Aquinas' systematic theology influenced the church and continues to remain at the heart of much of Catholic theology today. The host and the cup became such awesome vehicles of God's grace that concern for proper reception overruled any thought that infants and children must have the Sacrament for their salvation. What if a child should receive the Sacrament without understanding its significance? His writings refer to the words of Pope Melchiades, which are really from Faustus' homily!

> The Holy Ghost bestows at the font the fullness of innocence; but in Confirmation, He confers an increase in grace. Man is spiritually advanced by this sacrament to a perfect age.[30]

---

28. Bray, in Cully, ed., *Confirmation Re-Examined*, 49.

29. Fisher, "Confirmation: Then and Now," 135.

30. Price and Weil, *Liturgy for Living*, revised ed., 121.

In *Summa Theologica III3a.72.8*, he describes Confirmation as a "sacrament of maturity," bringing an increase of grace for a different phase of life.[31]

In Baptism, the Holy Spirit worked externally for regeneration and adoption; in Confirmation, the Holy Spirit was an internal effect that strengthened for Christian discipleship, allowing the presence (given at Baptism) to become more effective. This increase of grace (*augmentium gratiae*) gave strength (*robur*) to live and fight the battles of the Christian life, or spiritual warfare (*confirmamur ad pugnam*).[32] The kiss of peace at the end of the ceremony was replaced with a slap on the cheek,[33] a Roman practice closely associated with medieval guild practice used in commissioning and sending forth journeymen. Here emerged a distinct rite, separate from baptism, as a sacrament of the Holy Spirit for an increase of grace, strength to live and fight the battles of the Christian life, a sacrament of maturity. This reflects a synthesis of the Roman episcopal post-baptismal rites of hand laying with prayer and anointing, and the Spanish-Gallican practice of episcopal oversight and supervision of baptism called "confirmation."

At the Council of Cologne in 1280 it was declared that children under seven were too young to be confirmed, because one should learn the rudiments of faith in preparation: the Creed, the Lord's Prayer, and the Ave Maria. It is apparent that confirmation was being changed from being a sacrament of initiation to one with catechetical dimensions associated with an appropriate age.

Archbishop of Canterbury John Peckham issued a canon in 1282 requiring that Confirmation be the prerequisite to receiving communion. His aim was to rescue Confirmation from "damnable negligence" because bishops were not visiting parishes for Confirmation. It had the opposite effect. Daniel Stevick notes, "Gradually but inevitably, Confirmation in the West became the privilege of the few rather than the obligation of many."[34] What had become a source of strength had become a closed gate to fellowship. This medieval theology and practice of confirmation was canonized at the Council of Florence in 1439, in a *Decree for the*

---

31. Price, *Baptism & Ministry*, 89.

32. Charles U. Harris, "The Anglican Understanding of Confirmation," in Cully, ed., *Confirmation: History, Doctrine and Practice*, 21.

33. John Hill, "Some Disputed Questions About Confirmation" *Pacifica 11* (October 1998), 284.

34. Stevick, *Baptismal Moments*, 17.

Armenians, officially stating that in confirmation Christians grow in grace and are strengthened in faith.[35] The "age of discretion" was the key to a child's admittance to communion; a child was then old enough to know the difference between the sacramental meal and the family meal.

The Protestant Reformation returned to the understanding that baptism was complete in and of itself; there was new birth in water and the Holy Spirit. Paul Turner calls the meaning and practice of confirmation one of the controversies of the sixteenth century as the Church struggled to interpret the meaning and importance of the sacraments. He believes that although the origins of confirmation are with initiation, making it more a seal than strength, he agrees with the Reformers that baptism is so powerful a sacrament that it does not need to be sealed. For him, the seal of grace at baptism is the pouring out of grace of the Holy Spirit.[36]

Most Reformers were interested in a period of catechetical instruction done in relationship to an examination of the faith of children afterwards. A catechism became the official and common vehicle of instruction to prepare candidates. The Lutherans, Reformed, Anglicans, and Roman Catholics (after Trent) all used catechisms, with the English Catechism first appearing in the 1549 Prayer Book.[37]

The English Reformation (1534–1662) left the Church of England with a less than clear and definite process of Christian initiation. Baptism was a rite of infancy, followed by Catechism and Confirmation, normally at 14–16 years, followed by First Communion. Admission to communion was seen as the response to a communicant making a public profession of faith—not an integral part of sacramental initiation.[38] Water baptism was the full initiation while Confirmation was a pastoral rite. Baptismal vows were reaffirmed by those who had been baptized in infancy, with candidates taking on full responsibility of church membership as they received the laying on of hands from the chief pastor, the bishop, with a prayer for strengthening by the Holy Spirit for their new responsibilities.

---

35. Thomas Marsh, "Christian Initiation: Practice and Theology," *Confirming the Faith of Adolescents: An Alternative Future for Confirmation* (New York: Paulist Press, 1991), 13.

36. Paul Turner, *The Meaning and Practice of Confirmation: Perspectives from a Sixteenth-Century Controversy* (New York: Peter Lang Publishing, 1987), 326.

37. Imri M. Blackburn, "The Development of Confirmation Instruction in the Protestant Episcopal Church," in Cully, ed., *Confirmation: History, Doctrine and Practice*, 55.

38. Reginald H. Fuller, "Confirmation in the Episcopal Church and in the Church of England," in Cully, ed., *Confirmation Re-Examined*, 11.

As Archbishop of Canterbury, Thomas Cranmer authored the 1549 Book of Common Prayer, with Confirmation a rite reserved exclusively to the bishop; its theological emphasis was on the gift of the Holy Spirit, for strength and constancy.[39] Cranmer discarded the anointing, kept the hand-laying, and transposed confirmation to serve as a way for adolescents to mark the completion of catechizing.[40] According to Gerard Austin, Cranmer believed the Holy Spirit was given in baptism, confirmation was a catechetical process, signifying the coming of age in the life of faith.[41] The anointing with oil is omitted for the first time since apostolic times in the rite of Baptism,[42] and the final rubric states, "And there shall none be admitted to the Holy Communion until such time as he be Confirmed."[43] Cranmer's prayer books therefore made baptism the first stage of a two-part initiatory process. At the International Anglican Liturgical Consultation held in Boston in July 1985, it was acknowledged that Cranmer had shifted the emphasis of an outward rite to a catechizing event that had lost its sacramentality,[44] and the 1991 International Anglican Liturgical Consultation stated that baptism is complete sacramental initiation, including the gift of the Holy Spirit.[45]

Confirmation was meant to provide children who had come to "years of discretion" (regarded as around 10 to 12 years of age) with a ritual occasion in which they might ratify the promises of baptism "with their own mouth, and with their own consent, openly before the Church."[46] Anointing had been replaced by the laying on of hands—a gesture from the New Testament to mean bonding, blessing, commissioning, and healing. This became the outward and visible sign of the bishop's ministry of Confirmation. The 1552 BCP changes the prayer from "Send down . . ." to "Strengthen . . ." and an additional non-sacramental prayer is said for

---

39. Harris, in Cully, ed., *Confirmation: History, Doctrine and Practice*, 22.

40. James F. Turrell, *Celebrating the Rites of Initiation: A Practical Guide for Clergy and Other Liturgical Ministers* (New York: Church Publishing, 2013), 3.

41. Austin, *Anointing with the Spirit—The Rite of Confirmation*, 70.

42. Harris, in Cully, ed., *Confirmation: History, Doctrine and Practice*, 21.

43. Children's Committee, *Children and the Holy Communion: Guidelines and Resources for Parishes* (The Church in Wales: Council for Mission and Ministry, 2002), 7.

44. "Children and Communion," *Children at the Table: The Communion of All the Baptized in Anglicanism Today* (New York: The Church Hymnal Corporation, 1995), 133.

45. Meyers, "By Water and the Holy Spirit," 420.

46. Stevick, *Baptismal Moments*, 20.

spiritual growth, "Defend O Lord, this child with thy heavenly grace, that he . . . may . . . daily increase in the Holy Spirit . . ."[47] This strengthening appears to assume that the Holy Spirit has been given at baptism, and its presence is called upon for new vitality. A dismissal is pronounced with a prayer that mentions the bishop as successor of the apostles in regard to their ability to communicate the Holy Spirit.[48]

The Reformation continued to add to the meaning of Confirmation: increase of grace, power to preach to others, spiritual maturity, and strength for battle in the Christian life. Its delay after baptism saw confirmation as the ratification by an adult to the baptismal promises made on one's behalf when one was an infant. However, while Confirmation was ostensibly required by the prayer book, it was widely ignored in practice until the 1680s.

In Colonial America, Samuel Seabury, consecrated Bishop in 1784, emphasized the importance of Confirmation in his address at the first Connecticut Convention. *Canon 3* adopted in 1789 required regular and frequent Episcopal visitations and administration of Confirmation, and *Canon 11* stated that one of the duties of a minister was to "prepare children and others" for Confirmation, and at the bishop's visitation the minister was to be ready to present those "previously instructed for the same."[49] The Catechism was adopted as part of the American Book of Common Prayer, following closely to the prayer book of the Church of England. Confirmation was to be administered to baptized persons of competent age when they could say the Creed, the Lord's Prayer, and the Ten Commandments, and repeat answers from the Catechism with some understanding of meaning.

John Henry Hobart, Bishop of New York beginning in 1811, focused on the ministry of confirmation as part of his pastoral episcopate. He set the model for modern practice of Confirmation of the Episcopal Church by confirming those new to the Episcopal Church and expecting those Episcopalians who had not been confirmed to come for an episcopal blessing.[50] Hobart had a high view of the Church, and his view of

---

47. Children's Committee, *Children and the Holy Communion*, 7.

48. Price and Weil, *Liturgy for Living*, revised ed., 82.

49. Blackburn, in Cully, ed., *Confirmation: History, Doctrine and Practice*, 60–61.

50. Stevick, *Baptismal Moments*, 25.

Confirmation was of a rite of apostolic origin, divinely ordained as noted in Acts 8 and the writings of Tertullian, Cyprian, Jerome, Luther, and Calvin. He felt it was important for candidates to have a knowledge and meaning of the Catechism and an understanding of the plan of salvation.

Confirmation emerged as a sign of membership in the Episcopal Church because the United States had varied Protestant religious values, historically and geographically.[51] Finding itself in the midst of an American culture of various denominations that had rejected the practice of confirmation, a biblical foundation was necessary to explain this sacramental sign for the Episcopal Church. From 1892 through 1928, the Book of Common Prayer's Rite of Confirmation included the lesson from Acts 8:14–17. Many Episcopalians might have thought of this passage as describing their own church—the local priest baptizes and at a later time the bishop, representing the apostolic ministry, confers the Holy Spirit by the laying on of hands.

The 1928 BCP had lengthy rubrics regarding the responsibility of parents to bring their children to be baptized. Following baptism with water, the minister made the sign of the cross upon the child's forehead while praying that he shall not be ashamed to confess the faith of Christ crucified and to fight under his banner against sin, the world, and the devil, now being Christ's faithful soldier.[52] Following the Service of Baptism, Offices of Instruction were located in the Prayer Book, which could be used during worship, or as the rubrics admonish, for the clergy to instruct the young in preparation for confirmation.

Until the present use of the 1979 BCP, the Episcopal Church followed this model of Christian initiation: baptism in infancy, clergy-led education using the Offices of Instruction, followed by the laying on of hands by a bishop, then being welcomed as an adult member to receive Holy Communion for the first time. What was originally one initiation rite in the early Church had become three separate rites of initiation into the faith community.

---

51. Louis Weil, "American Perspectives: (ii) Confirmation," *Children at the Table: The Communion of All the Baptized in Anglicanism Today* (New York: The Church Hymnal Corporation, 1995), 71.

52. BCP 1928, 280.

CHAPTER 2

Liturgical Renewal
of Christian Initiation Rites

From about 1890 until 1970, a school of thought, popularly known as the "Mason-Dix" line, held the view that confirmation was the second and completing half of the full sacrament of initiation. It made a distinction between baptism of water, which provided cleansing from sin, and baptism of the Spirit, bestowed through the imposition of hands. This view insisted that the Spirit was active not in baptism, but in confirmation; the seal of the Spirit that completed Christian initiation.[1] Dom Gregory Dix in 1946 published *The Theology of Confirmation in Relation to Baptism*, in which he maintained that Confirmation was a rite taken from the New Testament,[2] consisting of a sealing with chrism—the outward sign of the sealing of the Spirit until the day of redemption. He advocated a revision of the doctrine of confirmation, calling for no interval of time between baptism and confirmation.

In 1951, G. W. Lampe published *The Seal of the Spirit*.[3] He argued that Confirmation was a post-apostolic rite for strengthening those baptized in infancy with the Holy Ghost the Comforter. He insisted that since membership in Christ is given by faith in the sacrament of baptism, baptism mediates the indwelling presence of the Spirit that also dwelt within Christ. The blessings of initiation are given at baptism, which is unrepeatable and rooted in the New Testament and early church liturgies. Baptism is itself the "seal." He felt that Confirmation should be administered as close to baptism as possible, with the ratification of baptismal promises of pastoral value. Leonel L. Mitchell agrees that one is sealed by

---

1. Ruth A. Meyers, "By Water and the Holy Spirit: Baptism and Confirmation in Anglicanism," *Anglican Theological Review* 83 (2001), 417.

2. Fisher, "Confirmation: Then and Now," 147.

3. G. W. H. Lampe, *The Seal of the Spirit* (London: Longmans, Green and Co., 1951), 305.

the Holy Spirit in baptism, whether it is the seal of consignation or the inward grace of the washing.[4]

Various doctrinal commissions and reports over the past thirty years have studied these two schools of thought in regard to confirmation. It has been largely agreed that baptism alone is complete initiation and fully admits a person (child or adult) to communion. Confirmation/laying on of hands has a pastoral role in the renewal of faith among the baptized and should no longer be seen as a requisite for communion.

The Episcopal Church struggled with the development of new rites to reflect this understanding. In the *Introduction to Prayer Book Studies 18*, it was explained, "The basic principle of this proposal is the reunion of Baptism, Confirmation, and Communion into a single, continuous service, as it was in the primitive Church."[5] Urban T. Holmes, a member of the Drafting Committee (1974–1976), argued that the description of confirmation as an adult affirmation of baptism was not consistent with the typical church practice of confirming young people at ages 9–12, calling the current practice "modern individualism" and "Pelagianism" because grace was being given in relation to merit and free will.[6] Controversy continued on sacramental and pastoral grounds.

In 1970, the Liturgical Commission of the Episcopal Church published *Prayer Book Studies 18*, promoting a unified rite of baptism that then appeared in the *Services for Trial Use*.[7] In this rite, when candidates have been baptized, the bishop or priest, in full sight of the congregation prays, ". . . Sustain them, O Lord, with your Holy Spirit . . ." Then he or she lays a hand on each person's head and signs their forehead with the cross, using chrism if desired, and says, "*N.*, you are sealed by the Holy Spirit in baptism and marked as Christ's own for ever." With these words and actions, the sealing of the Spirit and the hand-laying are united in baptism. Confirmation was to be eliminated as a separate service, but this proved to be unacceptable because there was no provision for commitment to Christ at the years of discretion. At the 1970

---

4. Leonel L. Mitchell, *Praying Shapes Believing: A Theological Commentary on the Book of Common Prayer* (Ridgefield, CT: Morehouse Publishing, 1985), 114–115.

5. Ruth Meyers, *The Renewal of Christian Initiation in the Episcopal Church 1928–1979* (Notre Dame, IN: University of Notre Dame, 1992), 215.

6. Meyers, *The Renewal*, 262.

7. Fisher, "Confirmation: Then and Now," 151.

General Convention in Houston, the water baptism part of this rite was adopted as a trial rite, the "sealing" was to be omitted in the case of infants but used for adults, and experiments were encouraged with earlier or later ages for Confirmation.[8]

Two schools of thought emerged from these studies.[9] *Confirmation A* (as named by Charles Price) was the rejoining of confirmation to baptism. A *Form of Commitment to Christian Service* was developed as an opportunity for those baptized as infants to confess their faith in Christ as they reached an age of maturity and to receive the strengthening of the Spirit. This did not satisfy its detractors, citing a lack of representation of the whole church as represented in Episcopal polity with the bishop. In 1971 the House of Bishops issued the *Pocono Statement*[10] that spoke of the pastoral and catechetical side of confirmation. It stated that in Holy Baptism a person is made fully and completely a Christian and member of the Church. Confirmation was not to be regarded as a procedure of admission to Holy Communion, but a rite of mature affirmation of faith in the presence of the bishop and sealed by the laying on of hands.

A more formal rite of mature commitment was proposed in 1973 that included affirmation of baptismal vows and laying on of hands by the bishop. This was a new service, but titled "Confirmation" despite the possibility of misunderstanding (called *Confirmation B* by Price). Found in the 1979 Book of Common Prayer (within the Rite of Holy Baptism), the entire community is invited to recommit himself or herself to Christ, along with the candidate. A prayer is said for the renewal of what has already happened in baptism: forgiveness of sins, sealing with the Spirit, and binding to God's service. There are two prayer alternatives that can be said as the bishop lays hands upon each candidate. The prayer "Defend, O Lord, . . ." is included, as it has been in every Anglican Prayer Book since 1552, with the exception of the change of "child" to "servant." The other prayer speaks of an ongoing sustenance and strengthening by the Spirit:

> Strengthen, O Lord, your servant *N.* with your Holy Spirit; empower *him* for your service; and sustain *him* all the days of his life. Amen.

---

8. Fuller, in Cully, ed., *Confirmation Re-Examined*, 15.

9. Price, *Baptism & Ministry*, 90–91.

10. Weil, "American Perspectives: (ii) Confirmation," 74–75.

According to Leonel Mitchell, "Confirmation is the renewal of the baptismal covenant, not its completion. Confirmands affirm their baptismal commitment while God renews the covenant and empowers them with the Holy Spirit to fulfill their baptismal promises and live the baptismal life to which they are committed."[11] The rubrics continue to state that those baptized at an early age are expected, when prepared and ready, to make a mature public affirmation of their faith and receive the laying on of hands by the bishop.

Lifting up of the role of laity and ordering the life of the church around baptism, the "new" prayer book was quite explicit: one became a member of the church solely through baptism, with no other additional rite required; and a two-stage process of membership was no longer in place, with the baptized as "junior members and the confirmed as full members."[12]

The framers of the 1979 prayer book restored the early church's liturgy of initiation—water-baptism with the imposition of hands (and consignation), with the optional use of chrism. With the inclusion of the Baptismal Covenant in this prayer book, a lifelong commitment to discipleship was emphasized, with an opportunity to continually renew those promises as each new member of the church was welcomed. Baptism is full initiation into the Body of Christ. Full membership.

---

11. Mitchell, *Praying Shapes Believing*, 119.
12. Turrell, *Celebrating the Rites of Initiation*, 7.

CHAPTER 3

Christian Initiation
and the Adolescent

Adolescence as we know it is a twentieth century phenomenon. Derived from the Latin *adolescere*, "to grow up," it usually refers to anyone who has reached puberty but who has not yet made the vocational, ideological, or relational commitments of young adulthood. The primary developmental task of adolescence is forming a definition of self, a coherent personal identity, a connection between the young person of childhood and the adult they hope to become. An identity includes the internal, self-constructed abilities, beliefs, attitudes, and individual history that give a person a sense of their own uniqueness and their sense of relationship to others. Mary Pipher describes the adolescent as a "traveler, far from home with no native land, neither children nor adults. Sometimes they are four years old, an hour later they are twenty-five. They don't really fit anywhere. There's a yearning for place, a search for solid ground."[1] The consistent issue of adolescent development is that of change—physical, emotional, academic, social, and spiritual.

As we have moved into the twenty-first century, cultural changes have impacted the nature of adolescence. Our postmodern, technological, and urbanized context affects the adolescent journey, and the passing on of faith via our traditional means of youth ministry is becoming increasingly difficult. Many accepted developmental theories, developed primarily in the mid-twentieth century, tend to view the adolescent journey as a relatively stable, predictable, and orderly—though sometimes difficult—process. For the past two or three decades, researchers and theorists attempting to more fully understand human development have

---

1. Mary Pipher, *Reviving Ophelia: Saving the Selves of Adolescent Girls* (New York: Ballantine Books, 1994), 52.

been challenging many of these "tidy" themes and stages of development. But postmodern culture has shown a shift in cultural values and structure, changes in the family system, new research into peer relations, and gender and ethnic differences; and new ways of thinking about morality, character, and ethics have become increasingly important in describing the nature of adolescence.[2]

Intellectually, adolescents live in two worlds at once—concrete experience and abstract thinking. According to Jean Piaget's theories, during the "concrete operational stage" (ages 7–11), there is an increased ability in classifying concrete objects and grasping concepts involved with mathematics, geography, and history. Some preadolescents (11–14 years) are in transition to the "formal operations stage," when they are able to think abstractly and imagine a world that might be. Psychologist Robert Kegan describes this new ability of thinking:

> This rebalancing, often the hallmark of adolescence, unhinges the concrete world. Where before the "actual" was everything, it falls away like the flats of a theater set, and a whole new world, a world the person never knew existed, is revealed. The actual becomes but one instance (and often one not very interesting instance) of the infinite array of the "possible" . . .[3]

By middle and late adolescence, youth have had more opportunity to test out their newly reasoned ideas against the real world and more balanced thought returns. Piaget views abstract thinking as being the product of both nature (brain cell development) and nurture (formal and informal education that enables the person to use newly acquired skills).[4] Beginning around the age of 16, the ability to respond differently to questions takes on a more intellectual framework. "Adult" thinking begins to take root.

Erik Erikson's stages of opposing forces of the human cycle focus on "Identity vs. Identity Confusion" during adolescence. Children are learning who they are and what direction their lives might take. In the first level of this stage, "identity diffusion/confusion," there is no coherent sense of self.

---

2. Kenda Creasy Dean, Chap Clark, and Dave Rahn, eds., *Starting Right: Thinking Theologically About Youth Ministry* (Grand Rapids, MI: Zondervan, 2001), 43.

3. Diane J. Hymans, "Adolescent Development," in Arthur J. Kubrick, ed., *Confirming the Faith of Adolescents: An Alternative Future for Confirmation* (New York: Paulist Press, 1991), 206.

4. Lois Sibley, ed., *Called to Teach and Learn: A Catechetical Guide for the Episcopal Church* (New York: The Domestic and Foreign Missionary Society PECUSA, 1994), 162–63.

The individual may seem aimless and uncommitted to a system of beliefs or values. They are often open to outside influences, which may or may not be healthy ones, and there is no resolution to making any significant ownership to identity. Next comes "experimentation," a moratorium period of trying on new roles and opinions that can come from parents, peers, other adults and role models, and the culture at large. It often involves living in crisis while attempting to resolve and examine a variety of life options. "Identity formation" involves self-choice, commitment, and consolidation of all that has been explored previously, with identity issues resolved independently as opposed to adopting those of parents. One becomes comfortable with one's sexual identity—discovering one's identity as a male or female in the context of what society teaches about such roles. A personal investment in and allegiance to a particular system of beliefs is self-chosen.

Erikson saw religious identity as a source of support and integration for various parts of this identity formation. Ideological commitment includes many factors, such as political, social, economic, social, and moral ideologies, with religious ideology being central to adolescents' commitment to them.[5] Donald Ratcliff also believes this quest involves the basic questioning of society, religious faith, and the values of the parental home.[6] A clear sense of personal identity is a prerequisite for the stage that follows, *Intimacy vs. Isolation*, which allows a person to enter into healthy relationships with others.

Carol Gilligan believes that intimacy and identity formation are more closely linked.[7] In her research she discovered that while men forge their identities through separation from others, women define themselves through their relationships and their ability to maintain them, with girls needing to maintain relationships masking their true opinions and feelings in order to do what they think is necessary to stay connected with others. James Marcia identifies late adolescence (ages 18–21) as this time of crisis and commitment.[8] He identifies an additional stage, "foreclosure," when one's beliefs and commitments are fixed and not open to question or

---

5. Shraga Fisherman, "Spiritual Identity in Israeli Religious Male Adolescents: Observations and Educational Implications," *Religious Education* 97 (2002), 62.

6. Donald Ratcliff, "Psychological Foundations of Multicultural Religious Education," in *Multicultural Religious Education* (Birmingham, AL: Religious Education Press, 1997), 121.

7. Carol Gilligan, *In a Different Voice: Psychological Theory and Women's Development* (Cambridge, MA: Harvard University Press, 1982).

8. Elizabeth F. Caldwell, *Leaving Home with Faith: Nurturing the Spiritual Life of Our Youth* (Cleveland, OH: The Pilgrim Press, 2002), 38.

examination. The individual commits to a set of goals and beliefs that are identical to those of their parents or others in authority, a result of socialization or indoctrination into a system sanctioned by others.

Adolescence is also a time of physical growth, with metabolism running the spectrum of boundless energy to total lethargy. Physical development will not necessarily indicate emotional or social development. Recent research from the National Institute of Mental Health[9] has shown that the prefrontal cortex of the brain, where emotional control, restraint of impulses, and rational decision-making abilities reside, experiences its greatest growth during adolescence. One researcher has said that this part of the brain enables us to live with ourselves and to function in society.[10] Young people must also cope with bodies that are maturing sexually while socially they are immature and in a state of dependence on the adults around them. This biosocial dilemma changes power relations, as any parent will share in speaking about their "authority" relationship with their teenage child.

Culture is related to issues of adolescent identity: vocation, sexuality, and a belief and value system. Today, electronic media provide our youth with information as to who they are, how they should look, and how they should behave. Margaret Mead has called this a *configurative culture*[11]— when young people learn more about life from peers than they do from their elders. Information is transferred horizontally within generations instead of vertically across generations. Education and work also separate adolescents and adults now more than ever, dividing the generations and making the peer group more influential. While biology signals the beginning of puberty, we tend to use social markers to indicate when it ends, many determined by the culture we live in.

Russian developmentalist Lev S. Vygotsky's (1896–1934) concept of development is that the formation of the mind is dependent on the social context in which an individual lives. James Riley Estep, Jr. uses Vygotsky's theories as a lens for understanding spiritual formation, understanding that Christian growth occurs within the developmental process.[12] Estep

9. Caldwell, *Leaving Home with Faith*, 22.

10. Michael Cole and Sheila R. Cole, *The Development of Children*, 3rd ed. New York: W.H. Freeman and Company, 1996, 64.

11. Hymans, in Kubrick, ed., *Confirming the Faith of Adolescents*, 207–11.

12. James Riley Estep, Jr., "Spiritual Formation as Social: Toward a Vygotskyan Developmental Perspective," *Religious Education* 97 (2002), 141–62.

proposes that intentional and unintentional instruction by a church community contributes to the spiritual formation of children; everyone impacts a child's understanding of God by how the Gospel is shared and lived out in community. For young people to grow and reach their formative potential, they must be in relationship with adults who have a strong faith identity, and are able to articulate it through word and action.

Faith is also in transition during adolescence. James Fowler (1981) describes adolescence as a time when they begin to see themselves as others see them.[13] His Stage 3: "Synthetic-Conventional Faith" (typically 11–13 years of age) involves asking questions and the search for truth. Thinking continues to mirror that of the community. God is seen in anthropomorphic terms, and moral reciprocity provides the basis for a relationship with God and of God's relationship with the world. Their question, "What do I believe?" is related to the communities that they relate to. Gradually they develop a theological ethic and rational system of beliefs and practices as they move into Stage 4: "Individuative-Reflective Faith" (after 18 years of age). The older adolescent begins to reflect critically on the tradition they have acquired as they take seriously the burden of responsibility for their own commitments, lifestyles, beliefs, attitudes, and values. With their growing confidence, they enter a demythologizing stage, which is marked by doubt and rejection of earlier beliefs, leading to stronger, more independent faith formed out of their new sense of identity.

John Westerhoff describes pre-adolescents (and children) in terms of an "Affiliative Faith." It is a religion "of the heart" in which experiences of awe, wonder, and mystery develop a sense of the holy. The focus is on belonging, as the individual seeks to act with others in a community that has a clear sense of identity. There is a desire to feel wanted, needed, and accepted in participation of community activities. Authority at this stage is the story of the community, inspiring action and a way of life. "Searching Faith" generally occurs in late adolescence and early adulthood, exhibited by expressions of critical thinking while seeking knowledge from a variety of faith traditions. It is a religion "of the head" in which doubt, critical judgment, experimentation, and a commitment to ideologies are characteristic.

---

13. James W. Fowler, *Stages of Faith: The Psychology of Human Development and the Quest for Meaning* (San Francisco: HarperSanFrancisco, 1991), 172–173, 182–183.

Sharon Daloz Parks believes that the ability to see the world through someone else's eyes helps a young person develop their sense of self—a recognition that the emerging self is composed of inward as well as external qualities. Youth inquire after God, seeking a relationship, while also imagining what it might be like to participate in the perspective of God.[14] According to Chap Clark, most adolescents engage in "intuitive theology."[15] This involves beliefs and actions that "feel" right to the teenager, but they lack a conscious structure or story to be able to explain it. This reflection about the divine-human relationship cannot be explained rationally and through language, but it is part of their inner life. If youth have been involved in a religious community, they might have an "embedded theology" that includes the images, language, and religious story inherited from the faith community. Clark feels that both of these types of theologies are easily manipulated and don't hold up well to scrutiny when faced with a faith crisis. This can be seen in devout high school students who go off to college only to find their newfound critical thinking skills have allowed them to step back and evaluate their beliefs from another perspective. Students with embedded theologies say, "I believe . . . ,"while students with deliberate theologies say, "I believe, because. . . ." This questioning of adolescence can lead to God, even when God is unknown.

There are always exceptions. In Kenda Creasy Dean's writings about the marks of Christian maturity, she states, "Faith is not measured by the standards of identity formation,"[16] noting how some young people (such as those with Down syndrome and other developmental challenges) can be remarkably articulate about matters of faith.

Historically, the markers to show the transition from childhood to adulthood have included rites of passage (initiation rites) and specific training for children preparing to take on adult roles in society. "Rites" are repetitive, symbolic actions (of word and deed) that express and indicate the community's sacred story or myth. There are two kinds of rites: rites of intensification and rites of transition, passage, or life crisis. Once these

---

14. Kenda Creasy Dean, "Fessing Up: Owning Our Theological Commitments," in Dean, Clark, and Rahn, eds., *Starting Right*, 31.

15. Chap Clark, "The Changing Face of Adolescence: A Theological View of Human Development," in Dean, Clark, and Rahn, eds., *Starting Right*, 29–30.

16. Kenda Creasy Dean, *Almost Christian: What the Faith of Our Teenagers Is Telling the American Church* (New York: Oxford University Press, 2010), 79.

rites and training are completed, the child is both equipped and expected to fulfill the role of an adult in his or her community. Christian initiation as defined by Mircea Eliade (and Mitchell) is "a body of rites and oral teachings whose purpose is to produce a decisive alteration in the religious and social status of the person to be initiated."[17] It is understandable to see how these two terms, rooted in religion and culture, have blended together.

A rite of passage has three parts, which Amanda Hughes and David Crean have used in developing *The Journey to Adulthood*[18] program of adolescent Christian formation:

1. A separation ceremony followed by a physical withdrawal from the community,

2. A period of transition in which a person experiences liminality that may include instructions in customs and history of the community as well as a physical ordeal that serves to bind the individual into the community with others who share and have shared the experience. Persons are formed and prepared for their new condition, acquiring the skills and knowledge needed for their new role, and

3. A rite of reincorporation. This is a ceremonial in which the person is re-established in the community with new responsibilities, new adult status, and often with a new name. This rite involves the whole community.

Modern American society (and the church) does not have anything that corresponds to a full initiation ceremony to make the passage out of childhood, so for many, Confirmation has taken this cultural role, although many say it has served as a graduation rite from the church.

For Episcopalians, this decisive change occurs in Holy Baptism, which is full initiation by water and the Holy Spirit into Christ's Body the Church. *Prayer Book Studies 18*[19] lists five factors that contribute to a person's becoming a Christian: Baptism, the family, the community, growing in relation to God, and renewal. While we are made full members at baptism, our faith formation involves a lifelong journey.

---

17. Mitchell, *Praying Shapes Believing*, 88.

18. David E. Crean, "Journey to Adulthood," in Sheryl A. Kujawa, ed., *Disorganized Religion: The Evangelization of Youth and Young Adults* (Boston: Cowley Publications, 1998), 125.

19. *Holy Baptism with the Laying-on-of-Hands: Prayer Book Studies 18 on Baptism and Confirmation* (New York: The Church Pension Fund, 1970), 29.

CHAPTER 4

The Catechumenate

For the past several hundred years, confirmation has been the final information-conveying educational process and/or indoctrination into a denomination's version of the Christian faith. The priest or other authority was the teacher who bestowed the necessary information, and the young people were the recipients who were taught how to give back information in the form of recitations and statements of faith. Confirmation programs kept young people in the church until their requirements were completed, then they were given the adult choice as to their participation in membership or not. According to the *Search Institute*, most did not come back.[1] There was no connection confirming what had taken place at baptism. It might be said that a mature commitment of faith by an adolescent within the framework of the laying on of hands by a bishop became an oxymoron. Understanding the development of an adolescent, it is not surprising to find that they are unable to make a commitment to a set of beliefs while still trying to identify one's self in relation to others, including God.

Catechesis is the process by which persons are continually formed as Christians within the life of a community of faith. It includes three inter-related processes that touch upon every phase and action associated with a faith community; "instruction"—the teaching processes in which the skills and knowledge that are important to the Christian life are shared; "education"—the process of critical reflection and participation and practice in regard to the life of Christ; and "formation"—how we participate in living a Christian life, supported and transformed by our actions and those of others as we continue to grow and learn more about ourselves, each other, and God. Catechesis is more than preparation for the sacraments or learning the Biblical story. It is connected to the ongoing life of a Christian, involving service and mission. Aristotle would have described

---

1. David Ng, "Rethinking Youth Ministry," in David S. Schuller, ed., *Rethinking Christian Education: Explorations in Theory and Practice* (St. Louis, MO: Chalice Press, 1992), 96.

it as *praxis*, the integration of *theoria* (knowledge for knowledge's sake) and *poiesis* (action).[2] For confirmation preparation, we are preparing for the apostolic life that involves a relationship of catechesis—from liturgical action and experience, followed by reflection, to apostolic action and reflection, back to liturgical action and reflection.

The catechumenal process is an ancient pattern for initiating Christians. The Catechumenate was a period of time that included participation in worship, Scripture study, development of a disciplined life of prayer, participation in helping those in need, one's daily ministry, tithing, and all the rites of the Church. Following baptism, a period of *mystagogia* was followed in which the newly baptized Christians (neophytes) were instructed in how to live the Christian life. They often took the form of homilies on baptism, anointing, and Eucharist.[3]

The word catechumen comes from a Greek word meaning "to sound in the ear." Thus, the catechumenal process is not one of learning by rote. It is the "sounding in the ear" of the Word of God, the deep hearing of God's will by a believer. The Word of God reaches its fullest expression in Jesus Christ, "the Word made flesh." Therefore, the catechumenal process is Word-centered. At the heart of its study is hearing the Word of God in our Sunday readings, bolstered by worship, story-sharing, group study, service, working for social justice—in other words, living out those promises made in our Baptismal Covenant to become doers of the Word. Louis Weil, a long-time proponent of reviving the catechumenate, speaks of the process "as offering people a chance to make an affective as well as an intellectual response to the Gospel."[4]

James Turrell encourages the Episcopal Church to reinvest in the catechumenal process for the unbaptized as well as those who are reaffirming their baptismal promises.[5] The catechumenate's emphasis on formation over information, on walking the walk of Christian life, and on the creation of supportive community in small groups and in sponsoring relationships

2. John H. Westerhoff III, "Aspects of Adult Confirmation," in Cully, ed., *Confirmation Re-Examined*, 117.

3. Mary Ann Hinsdale, "Infinite Openness to the Infinite," in Marsha J. Bunge, ed., *The Child in Christian Thought* (Grand Rapids, MI: Wm. B. Eerdmans Publishing Co., 2001), 418.

4. Office of Evangelism Ministries, The Episcopal Church Center, *The Catechumenal Process: Adult Initiation & Formation for Christian Life and Ministry* (New York: The Church Hymnal Corporation, 1990), 6.

5. Turrell, *Celebrating the Rites of Initiation*, 141.

works effectively for those seeking to reaffirm their vows as well as for those making their vows for the first time. It is not a time for cognitive learning about the Christian life, but a lived experience of that life. The Word of God should be central to one's style of life and affect everything one does within and outside the faith community. How did we lose this understanding in our practices of Christian initiation? Does today's Church find itself in circumstances similar to the ancient Christian communities?

Catechisms arose in an age when it was valid to presume that everyone was surrounded by Christian culture and were thus immersed in that religious experience. Many current confirmation curricula loosely follow denominational catechisms today, and many echo the old catechisms in offering theology instead of spirituality—telling the inquirer about God rather than nurturing them into a relationship with God. These can be found in many resources published as recently as the 1990s, with workbook approaches that students fill in the blanks with correct information that can be researched using a bible and prayer book.

In the early nineteenth century, the Sunday School became the primary context for catechesis and it fit well into the religious-minded society. Despite our religiously pluralistic and secular society in America today, the Church continues in large part to follow this traditional model of catechesis with adolescents. Classes are held with teachers and learners gathered over books and papers, lectures, with homework given, a video shown, or scripture studied.

To be serious about Christian formation today means asking ourselves how we educate our children, how we prepare young people for adult reaffirmation, how we prepare converts (unbaptized) to membership, and how we encourage people in their continuing growth and formation as Christians—whether it be from the Episcopal tradition or any other Christian tradition for reception into the Episcopal Church.

There are three processes outlined in *The Book of Occasional Services* (BOS):[6]

1. For Unbaptized Adults

    a. Pre-Catechumenal or Inquiry Period
    b. The Catechumenate

---

6. *Book of Occasional Services 2003* (New York: Church Publishing, 2004), 114–126, 136–139, 157–162.

    c. Candidacy for Baptism

    d. Following Baptism

2. For Reaffirmation of Baptismal Vows

    a. Inquiry

    b. Deeper Exploration of Faith and Ministry

    c. Preparation for Reaffirmation

    d. Reaffirmation

3. Preparation of Parents and Godparents for the Baptism of Infants and Young Children

    a. Blessing of Parents and the Choosing of Godparents

    b. Preparation for Baptism

    c. Child's Formation in Salvation History, Prayer, Worship, and Social Ministry (carried out by parents, godparents, and the congregation)

Today, if congregations became "catechetical communities" of lifelong learning in which pre- and post-baptismal catechesis were infused into the congregation, the mission of the Church would be understood by "old" members as well as "new." Each individual would understand their baptismal promises to support each other in their life of faith, and the traditions of the faith would be taught and caught by its youngest members.

The twenty-first century is a post-Christian era; modeling our initiation rites (and preparation for them) on the early Church can only strengthen our understanding of what a "renewed commitment to Christ" really means. As faith communities live out God's mission, the pattern of Christian formation provided by the catechumenal process will become an invaluable tool.

PART II

A PUBLIC AFFIRMATION

The gifts he gave were that some would be apostles, some prophets, some evangelists, some pastors and teachers, to equip the saints for the work of ministry, for building up the body of Christ, until all of us come to the unity of the faith and of the knowledge of the Son of God, to maturity, to the measure of the full stature of Christ.

—Ephesians 4:11–13

CHAPTER 5

Re-Imagining Confirmation

Ruth A. Meyers

Among the myriad changes in the 1979 Book of Common Prayer, none are more profound, more far reaching, than those in the rites and practices of what is frequently called "Christian initiation": baptism, confirmation, and admission to communion. Moreover, in the nearly four decades since the book was introduced, none of the changes has resulted in more confusion and disagreement than the rite of Confirmation, with forms for Reception and for the Reaffirmation of Baptismal Vows.

Each year, I begin a seminary class session on confirmation by asking students to tell one another the story of their confirmation, reception, or adult baptism in the Episcopal Church. Were you, for example, baptized as an infant in the Episcopal Church and later confirmed, or did you affiliate with the Episcopal Church after being an active member of another church? What preparation and follow-up did you have? Was the rite part of your regular parish Sunday Eucharist, or a diocesan service gathering people from many different congregations? How did this liturgy relate to your admission to communion?

Every time I use this exercise, students are astonished to hear one another's stories. Those baptized when the 1928 prayer book was in use recall waiting until they were confirmed to be admitted to communion. Some were required to be confirmed when they became Episcopalians, even though they had undergone extensive preparation and been confirmed as a teenager in a Lutheran congregation. Others with a similar background were received rather than confirmed, some with laying on of hands, others without the ritual action. Those baptized as infants in the Episcopal Church report widely different ages at which they were confirmed; some ask why the bishop slapped them in addition to laying hands on their head. Occasionally a student reports participating in an extensive catechumenate leading to baptism as an adult, with no further rite of

Confirmation expected, while others baptized as adults were confirmed by their bishop soon after their baptism.

These widely divergent practices of confirmation and related rites reflect a lack of consensus in the Episcopal Church. In 1968, as prayer book revision was beginning, Frederick Warnecke, Bishop of Bethlehem (Pennsylvania), complained about the multiple meanings of confirmation as it was then practiced:

> [A] number of ill-assorted matters are packaged together in the grab-bag that we call Confirmation. There is the concept that Confirmation is the fulfillment of the commitment of Holy Baptism. There is the imagery of the reception of the sevenfold gifts of the Holy Spirit symbolized by the Laying on of Hands. There is the practical use of the service of Confirmation as a discipline of admission to the Holy Communion. Finally, this is all made the occasion of an episcopal visitation to a congregation and a church. These unlikely matters are intertwined in utter theological and practical confusion![1]

Apart from confirmation's purpose as a gateway to communion, Warnecke's comments could have been written today, despite the significant changes from the 1928 to the 1979 prayer book.

To unpack the "grab-bag" that is Confirmation in the Episcopal Church today, I begin with a review of the revisions of baptism and confirmation that led to the rites in the 1979 prayer book. The compromises made as the rites were developed have contributed significantly to the current lack of clarity. Exploring the theological, liturgical, and pastoral principles underlying the rite of Confirmation in the 1979 prayer book yields insights leading to a re-imagined, more coherent practice today.

FULL INITIATION BY WATER AND THE SPIRIT

The 1979 prayer book makes what at the time was a startling claim: "Holy Baptism is full initiation by water and the Holy Spirit into Christ's Body, the Church." For most of the twentieth century, Anglicans had debated the work of the Holy Spirit in baptism and confirmation. Some adopted

---

1. Frederick J. Warnecke, "A Bishop Proposes," in *Confirmation Crisis* (New York: Seabury Press, 1968), 136.

the position that A. J. Mason first articulated in the late nineteenth century and Gregory Dix developed in the mid-twentieth century: baptism, the first stage in the sequence of Christian initiation, effects cleansing from sin but is wholly incomplete without the seal of the Spirit bestowed in confirmation. Geoffrey Lampe, drawing upon many of the same sources from scripture and the early church, countered that the Spirit is fully at work in the waters of baptism, sealing the believer and marking the newly baptized as Christ's. Yet the benefits of baptism are only gradually realized over the course of Christian life, and for those baptized as infants, the effects are more potential than actual. Confirmation, Lampe argued, is a significant moment in a believer's realization of the baptismal seal but does not provide any special gift of the Spirit.

To underscore the work of the Spirit in baptism, the revisers included in the 1979 baptismal rite the classic prayer for the sevenfold gift of the Spirit, a prayer that had been part of confirmation in every Anglican prayer book since 1549. The formula that follows, "you are sealed by the Holy Spirit in Baptism and marked as Christ's own for ever," further emphasizes the Spirit's action in baptism. Some locate the bestowal of the Spirit in the waters of baptism, while others insist that the prayer and hand-laying with signing and chrismation constitute a distinct sacramental action associated with the gift of the Spirit. Yet regardless of the nuances of interpretation, it is one rite, effecting *full* initiation by water *and* the Spirit.

No longer is confirmation required for admission to communion. The confirmation rubric, "And there shall be none admitted to the Holy Communion, until such time as he be confirmed, or be ready and desirous to be confirmed," is no longer in the prayer book, replaced by a canon stipulating that baptism is the sacramental prerequisite to communion.

Confirmation, then, is not a rite of Christian initiation, incorporating believers into the body of Christ. In the 1979 BCP, Confirmation is a rite of renewal and reaffirmation, a part of Christian life rather than the completion of initiation into that life.

The Episcopal Church is not alone in this new approach to Christian initiation and reaffirmation of faith. "Principles of Christian Initiation," recommended in 1991 by the International Anglican Liturgical Consultation, affirm that baptism is complete sacramental initiation, leading to participation in the Eucharist, while Confirmation is a pastoral rite whose primary purpose is renewal of faith. A few provinces of the Anglican

Communion had already revised their liturgical books along these lines, and since the 1991 consultation, several other provinces have done so. Increasingly across the Anglican Communion, baptism is full Christian initiation and culminates in admission to communion. However, as in the Episcopal Church, understandings and practices of Confirmation continue to manifest theological confusion.

CONFIRMATION: COMMISSIONING FOR MINISTRY?

One way to interpret Confirmation is as a rite of commitment to ministry. Beginning in 1662, the Anglican Confirmation rite included a question asking candidates to renew the "solemn promise and vow" made at their baptism and thereby acknowledge themselves bound to "do all those things" that they, or their sponsors on their behalf, had undertaken at that time. Yet only in the early twentieth century did Anglican theologians begin to interpret this ratification of baptismal promises as a commissioning for ministry, describing Confirmation as a kind of ordination of the laity. In this view, Confirmation is not so much a sealing with the Holy Spirit as it is a particular enabling gift of the Spirit, strengthening confirmands for their ministry in the world.

This interpretation of Confirmation as ordination of the laity did not hold sway for long. By the late 1950s, some Anglicans were arguing instead that baptism be understood as ordination of the laity because it is incorporation into the priesthood of believers. These two perspectives have existed side by side for some time, continuing to this day.

In the revision process leading to the 1979 prayer book, the first proposal for Christian initiation, presented in 1968, eliminated Confirmation entirely. Renewal of the commitments made at baptism would occur when the congregation joined in the baptismal promises at each celebration of baptism. This proposed rite was published two years before the General Convention that would act on it, and response was swift. There were so many calls for a separate rite of reaffirmation of faith that the Standing Liturgical Commission introduced "A Form of Commitment to Christian Service" in a collection of pastoral offices published shortly before the 1970 General Convention. This rite was approved for trial use and eventually included in the 1979 Book of Common Prayer, although it does not seem to have been widely used, then or now.

Calls for a separate rite of reaffirmation of faith, presided over by a bishop, continued as the next round of prayer book revision got underway after the 1970 General Convention. The Theological Committee of the House of Bishops pressed the Standing Liturgical Commission to retain Confirmation as a distinctive rite of personal discipleship, sending individuals into the world. The Standing Liturgical Commission continued to insist that baptism is the foundation of Christian life, including commissioning for mission. Theological statements and proposals went back and forth, culminating in December 1972 with a meeting of the Standing Liturgical Commission, the Theological Committee of the House of Bishops, and the Prayer Book and Liturgy Committee of the House of Bishops. By the end of the meeting, the bishops had reached agreement on a series of theological principles concerning baptism and a post-baptismal affirmation of vows. With regard to baptism, the statement affirmed the sufficiency of baptism as full Christian initiation. While the essential element is baptism by water in the triune name, the bishops agreed, the rite also normatively includes "commissioning for Christian mission."

The 1979 baptismal rite unequivocally expresses these theological principles. Not only does the Baptismal Covenant conclude with questions inviting commitment to active Christian discipleship in the world—proclaiming the Gospel by word and example, seeking and serving Christ in all persons, striving for justice and peace—the Prayers for the Candidates ask God to "teach them to love others in the power of the Spirit" and "send them into the world in witness to your love." For adults and older children, this commitment to ministry begins to take shape even before the moment of baptism. The catechumenate in *The Book of Occasional Services* calls for reflection on "the catechumen's gifts for ministry and work for justice and peace." The assumption is that adults preparing for baptism already have gifts for ministry and that, even before they are baptized, they will begin a "practice of life in accordance with the Gospel (including service to the poor and those in need)."

The baptismal rite makes clear that this exercise of ministry requires God's enabling power as well as our active commitment. The Baptismal Covenant begins with the Apostles' Creed, a statement of belief in the triune God, revealed in creation, in the sending of Jesus, and in the work of the Holy Spirit. In response to God's self-offering, we commit ourselves to a particular way of life, one of worship and service, justice-making and reconciliation. In the Baptismal Covenant, we answer each question of commitment by saying, "I will, with God's help," indicating that Christian discipleship requires not just *our* commitment, *our* action, but also *God's* empowering Spirit. Following the Baptismal Covenant, we pray for the candidates, underscoring that the baptized are caught up in the movement of God's mercy and grace, offering ourselves in loving service because God first loved us.

While baptism fully commissions a person for Christian ministry, every Christian, at whatever age baptized, must grow into the full stature of Christ (Ephesians 4:13). For some, there may be a distinctive moment of new maturity in faith, when the eyes of one's heart (Ephesians 1:18) become open to the Spirit in a new way, resulting in a new depth of commitment to God's mission in the world. For these Christians, a ritual expression of their renewed commitment and of God's enabling Spirit, whether through Confirmation, or reaffirmation of faith, or A Form of Commitment to Christian Service, may be very appropriate. But such a ritual is not essential to Christian faith and life. Some Christians may never experience a unique moment of renewed or deepened grace and commitment, but instead find themselves steadily growing as Christians, more and more able to receive the gifts of the Spirit and manifest those gifts in their patterns of life. At what point should they be confirmed? More importantly, whether a Christian experiences a dramatic reawakening or a more gradual pattern of growth, this is a lifelong process.

Ritual expressions of the Spirit's strengthening grace can remind us of our dependence on God even as we renew our resolve to lead a Christian life. Some of these moments are regular parts of Christian life. The Easter Vigil provides an annual opportunity for members of the assembly to renew their baptismal vows, whether or not there are candidates for baptism, and a similar renewal may take place on other baptismal feasts. Moreover, every celebration of the Eucharist is a renewal of baptism. After receiving communion, the assembly gives thanks to God "for assuring us in these holy mysteries that we are living members of the Body of your Son," a membership bestowed in baptism, and we ask God to "send us out to do the work you have given us to do, to love and serve you as faithful witnesses of Christ our Lord," recalling the baptismal commitment to active Christian discipleship.

In addition to these regular occasions for renewing Christian commitment, the Book of Common Prayer sets forth the expectation that every member of the church, whether baptized at an early age or as an adult, make a commitment to the responsibilities of their baptism in the presence of a bishop. That this is a renewal or recommitment to the baptismal promises, not a new commissioning, is readily apparent for those baptized as adults, who make a conscious profession of faith and commitment to participate in ministries of justice and service. But what of those baptized as infants or young children? Certainly as they grow into adulthood, they are able to become more intentional in their Christian commitment. A ritual such as Confirmation provides opportunity for them to own the commitments made on their behalf by parents and godparents and to experience the empowering gift of the Spirit in their lives. Yet an emphasis on Confirmation as *the* distinctive rite that now sends them into the world in mission diminishes and distorts the Spirit's work in children and teenagers throughout the course of their development. True, the cognitive developments that occur during adolescence—abstract thinking, self-reflection, identity formation—allow the development of a system of beliefs and values, resulting in a more intentional Christian commitment. But living out the commitments to ministry made at one's baptism does not begin in adolescence.

Elementary-age children begin developmentally to use their physical and intellectual capacities to contribute productively to their world. This newly emerging sense of industry gives children at this stage particular interest in and energy for service to others. One group of children, a Sunday school class, began to correspond with children in Argentina, a connection made through a missionary. As their relationship developed, they organized a collection to meet the needs of their new friends in a faraway place. Such activity clearly embodies the baptismal commitment to mission. I am not proposing that these children should therefore be confirmed, but rather that we recognize their activity as a result of the Spirit empowering them for their service and as an expression of the Baptismal Covenant.

Moreover, even younger children have something to offer the Christian community. One young Christian I knew was a particularly enthusiastic worshiper. From infancy, her parents brought her regularly to the Eucharist, and by the time she was three, her "Amen" to the Eucharistic prayer rang out loudly in the assembly. I became accustomed to hearing her behind me during communion, asking whether it was her turn yet, eagerly awaiting the gift of Christ's Body and Blood. Her presence in that worshiping community was a witness to all of a joyous and unrestrained response to the incredible gift of God's love made tangible in the Eucharistic gifts.

In sum, rather than viewing Confirmation as a distinctive, unrepeatable rite of empowerment by the Spirit for commitment to Christian service, we need a fuller appreciation of the commissioning for mission that is integral to baptism. This is not just a matter of rhetoric, but of concrete expressions of the place of confirmation in the Episcopal Church.

Thirty years ago, the General Convention enacted a number of changes to the constitution and canons in light of the changes introduced in the 1979 prayer book. Prior to 1985, the canons required an Episcopalian to be a "communicant in good standing" in order to hold office or be ordained. The 1985 convention altered this language to "confirmed adult communicant." Before 1979, a communicant was by definition confirmed, since the effect of the "confirmation rubric" was to require confirmation for admission to communion. By continuing to require confirmation for various forms of ministry in the church, the convention rejected the theological principles underlying the 1979 prayer book, in particular the understanding that baptism commissions a person for ministry. Canonical revisions after 1985 likewise have required confirmation for various forms of service and ministry, including membership in church-wide commissions, lay liturgical ministries, and ordination. The 2012 General Convention considered a series of revisions to the constitution and canons that would eliminate the requirement for confirmation. After vigorous debate, convention referred the matter to the Standing Commission on Ministry Development.

Those who support the requirement generally cite the value of the conscious commitment made at Confirmation, whether a specific commitment to ministry or a broader affirmation of one's baptismal faith. Certainly it is appropriate to expect that those holding leadership positions in the church be faithful Christians, actively engaged in living out their baptismal commitments. Yet such commitment is better assessed as an ongoing pattern of life rather than on the basis of the one-time commitment made at Confirmation. The canons already define a communicant in good standing as one who is "faithful in corporate worship" and "faithful in working, praying, and giving for the spread of the Kingdom of God," and this is a sufficient standard by which to determine eligibility for leadership, whether lay or ordained.

CONFIRMATION: REAFFIRMATION OF FAITH?

In addition to making a commitment to the responsibilities of baptism, the rubrics introducing the 1979 rite of Confirmation, Reception, and Reaffirmation set forth an expectation that baptized Christians will make a mature public affirmation of faith. This public reaffirmation has been an explicit part of Anglican confirmation rites since 1662. In the 1979 prayer book, this reaffirmation is set within Christian faith and life and is not a rite subsequent to baptism that completes Christian initiation. Moreover, the 1979 book offers a much broader understanding of reaffirmation of faith.

Once the 1970 General Convention rejected the bold proposal to eliminate Confirmation altogether, theologians, bishops, and other church leaders began to consider the possibility of a repeatable rite of reaffirmation of faith. The December 1972 meeting of the Standing Liturgical Commission, the Theological Committee of the House of Bishops, and the Prayer Book and Liturgy Committee of the House of Bishops resulted in agreement not only about baptism but also concerning what was then called a "postbaptismal affirmation of vows." Such a rite could provide an opportunity for "mature personal acceptance of promises and affirmations made on one's behalf at infancy" and serve as well for other occasions, such as affiliation with the Episcopal Church and return to active Christian life after a period of lapsed or perfunctory faith.

Prayer book revision resulted in a rite that does much of what the bishops envisioned in 1972. The 1979 rite provides confirmation for those baptized as infants, reception of those affiliating with the Episcopal Church, and reaffirmation by any who want to reaffirm their baptismal vows. However, there are some important differences. The title "confirmation" was restored to prominence, over the objections of the Drafting Committee on Christian Initiation. The 1972 principles stated that the affirmation of faith by those baptized in infancy ought to be voluntary, though strongly encouraged; the introductory rubrics to the 1979 rite say that this affirmation is expected, and the canons require it for many positions of leadership. Most significantly, the 1976 General Convention added a rubric setting forth the expectation that those baptized as adults, unless baptized with laying on of hands by a bishop, are also expected to make an affirmation of faith in the presence of the bishop. By expecting a rite subsequent to baptism, this rubric undermines the sufficiency of baptism as full Christian initiation, and the canons that require this separate laying on of hands for leadership positions exacerbate the problem.

I propose that we reconsider the spirit of the 1972 agreed statement, which considers Confirmation and other postbaptismal rites of affirmation as pastoral rites. For those baptized as infants, such an affirmation is a "normal component of Christian nurture" and so is "pastorally and spiritually desirable." The prayer book, as well as the 1972 principles, describes this as a *mature* commitment. It is not a rite of puberty, suitable for children in early adolescence when they are just beginning the cognitive developments that accompany adolescence. Rather than focusing programs for teens on confirmation preparation, we must provide ongoing formation that supports development of their faith and encourages reflection on the implications of Christian faith for the challenges of daily living that teens face today.

Just as confirmation is pastorally desirable for those baptized as infants, a ritual reaffirmation of baptismal commitments is a suitable pastoral response on other occasions in Christian life. The 1991 Anglican liturgical consultation noted: "The laying on of hands, with prayer for further strengthening by the Spirit, is open to many uses. Such a 'stretched' rite, perhaps termed *commissioning* or *affirmation*, able to be repeated as different pastoral needs arise, and creatively adapted to various times and places, may bring new life to this distinctive Anglican heritage [i.e., confirmation]." The report continued, "The church long ago recognized that the journey of the baptized in their exploration of the life of faith is a process punctuated by failure and forgiveness, repentance and renewal."

With the introduction of a form for reaffirmation of baptismal vows, the 1979 BCP provides a ritual expression of renewed or deepened faith as one possible pastoral response to various Christian experiences. The canon on membership adopted in 1985 introduced a particular use of the reaffirmation. Needing to define "confirmed adult communicant," the canon lists several ways in which a person can be considered "both baptized and confirmed." Confirmation—that is, the use of a formula "For Confirmation"—is not expected for all members of the Episcopal Church. A person baptized as an adult who subsequently "receives the laying on of hands by the Bishop in Reaffirmation of Baptismal Vows" is considered to be both baptized and confirmed. That is, a bishop may use the formula "For Reaffirmation" rather than one "For Confirmation." This is a slight distinction, a tiny step away from "confirmation," narrowly defined, for someone who is baptized as an adult. However, the distinction has not been widely recognized or applied. In a 2005 survey of Episcopal bishops, most indicated that they use reaffirmation only for those already confirmed or received. Only two reported that they also use reaffirmation for those baptized as adults, although several said they reaffirm anyone who desires it or anyone the rector presents.

The canon also stipulates that a person "who is baptized in this Church as an adult and receives the laying on of hands by the Bishop at Baptism" is considered to be both baptized and confirmed. The laying on of hands at baptism uses neither a formula "For Confirmation" nor the one "For Reaffirmation." Rather, the canon refers to the action and formula that follow the water baptism: the presider lays a hand on the candidate's head while tracing the sign of the cross on the forehead ("consignation"), with the option of using chrism ("chrismation"), saying, "You are sealed by the Holy Spirit in Baptism and marked as Christ's own for ever." For adults baptized by a bishop, neither confirmation nor any other ritual action or affirmation is expected.

CONFIRMATION: THE ROLE OF THE BISHOP?

The canonical definitions of "baptized and confirmed" status highlight a significant feature of the 1979 rite for Confirmation, Reception, and Reaffirmation: the role of the bishop. As the prayer book was being revised, many Episcopalians were insistent on retaining this feature. For them, this ritual laying on of hands by a bishop is key to our Anglican identity.

Certainly Anglicans understand episcopacy to be essential. The Chicago-Lambeth Quadrilateral adopted at the end of the nineteenth century includes the historic episcopate as one of four elements that provide the basis for unity with other churches. These principles continue to guide our ecumenical dialogues; for example, resolving our differences on episcopacy was essential to achieving full communion with the Evangelical Lutheran Church in America.

Nonetheless, it is possible to maintain the historic episcopate without focusing that ministry in the liturgical rite of Confirmation and without requiring a bishop to administer Confirmation. Our sisters and brothers in Eastern Orthodox churches have never had a separate rite of Confirmation presided over by a bishop. Orthodox baptismal rites include anointing with chrism, using oil previously blessed by the patriarch, and Anglicans have considered this the equivalent of Confirmation when deciding to receive rather than confirm members of those churches. In the Roman Catholic Church, the Rite of Christian Initiation of Adults approved in 1972 expects that in the absence of a bishop, the priest who administers baptism will immediately confirm the newly baptized. Since these rites expect that adult initiation will occur at the Easter Vigil, the most common practice is for the parish priest to baptize and confirm adults. Moreover, the Roman Catholic Church allows a presbyter both to confirm in certain circumstances those baptized as infants and to confirm baptized adults who are received into full communion.

The practices of the Roman Catholic and Orthodox churches suggest that Anglicans might reconsider the bishop's role in Confirmation. The 1979 prayer book introduced a shift by identifying the bishop as the principal celebrant of baptism, and the 1991 International Anglican Liturgical Consultation encouraged a broader understanding of the bishop's ministry consistent with Anglican tradition. A bishop is chief priest and pastor, called to "encourage and support all baptized people in their gifts and ministries." As teacher of the faith, a bishop proclaims the Gospel, preaching the word and interpreting Scripture. As guardian of the faith and unity of the church, a bishop is a visible sign of the congregation's connections with the diocese and with the Episcopal Church and the Anglican Communion. It is within the wider context of the bishop's ministry that we should consider the bishop's liturgical roles. The 1991 Anglican liturgical consultation concluded that, whenever possible, the bishop should preside at baptism and Eucharist, and further that a bishop may delegate confirmation to a presbyter.

The 1979 prayer book places baptism as the foundation of the church's life. Focusing the bishop's liturgical ministry on Confirmation obscures the more fundamental sacrament of baptism. While a bishop cannot be present at every celebration of baptism, it is possible and even desirable that congregations schedule baptisms for the bishop's visit, whether or not there are also persons being presented for Confirmation, Reception, or Reaffirmation. When there is neither Baptism nor Confirmation, the Eucharist may include the Renewal of Baptismal Vows, and the verbal renewal can be accompanied by the Thanksgiving over the Water and sprinkling the congregation with the water.

Moreover, in planning a bishop's visit, it is important to consider not only the bishop's liturgical leadership but the entirety of the event. What sort of teaching and other interaction will best allow the bishop to support and encourage all the baptized in their ministries? How might the bishop's visit enable the congregation to deepen its relationship with the diocese and the wider church? While ritual has some power to shape Christian faith and life, it is most effective when we connect it to other experiences and relationships in our lives. There is power in a bishop ritually laying hands on a baptized person who has come to a place of renewed or deepened faith. There is even more power when that baptized person also has opportunity to reflect with the bishop on their gifts for ministry or to share some of their faith journey with the bishop.

CONFIRMATION: AFFILIATION WITH THE EPISCOPAL CHURCH?

Another argument sometimes advanced in favor of confirmation, including the requirement of confirmation for leadership positions, is the use of Confirmation as a rite of affiliation with the Episcopal Church. Prior to the 1979 prayer book, it was customary to confirm those coming from Protestant churches while receiving those who came from Roman Catholic and Orthodox churches. The distinction was not made on the basis of whether one's former church had a rite of Confirmation—Lutheran churches practiced confirmation, yet we confirmed Lutherans; in contrast, although Orthodox churches do not have a separate rite of Confirmation, we received rather than confirmed members of those churches. In each case, the deciding factor was whether an individual came from a church with the historic episcopate. If so, that person could be received, sometimes in a formal ceremony presided over by a bishop or priest, sometimes simply by being added to the congregation's roster of baptized and confirmed members.

The 1979 prayer book introduced a rite of reception parallel to Confirmation, the only difference from Confirmation being the bishop's words at the central ritual moment and the absence of a specific requirement for a ritual gesture to accompany the formula. But who is to be confirmed and who received? What ritual gesture is appropriate? Since 1979, no consistent understanding or practice has emerged. Should we continue to confirm Protestants and receive Catholics and Orthodox? Should we receive Protestants who have been confirmed in their previous tradition but confirm those who haven't, including those from churches, such as Baptist churches, that have no rite of Confirmation? Should we receive everyone regardless of their prior church affiliation, as long as they have been baptized? What are the implications of our full communion with the Evangelical Lutheran Church in America and with the Moravian Church? Is any rite, whether reception or Confirmation, to be expected when a person is from a body already in full communion with the Episcopal Church?

The 2005 survey of Episcopal bishops showed widely divergent practices. Many said that they receive those from Orthodox, Lutheran, and Roman Catholic churches, while others limited reception to those from Roman Catholic and Orthodox traditions. One receives those "who have made a mature affirmation in a church in communion" with the Episcopal Church. At the other end of the spectrum, at least twenty said they receive anyone who has made an adult commitment in another Christian tradition, and two would receive any baptized Christian from another church. One bishop said simply, "If present and desirous."

The canons haven't helped clarify the matter. The canon adopted in 1985 offers several options. A baptized person "who received the laying on of hands (by any Bishop in apostolic succession) and is received into the Episcopal Church by a bishop of this Church" is considered to be both baptized and confirmed. Although this is intended to maintain the historic practice of receiving Roman Catholics and Orthodox Christians, those churches do not require that the bishop be the one to lay hands on the person. Putting the phrase "by any Bishop in apostolic succession" in parentheses is a subtle acknowledgment of this reality, but it does not provide unambiguous guidance for interpreting the canon. The next paragraph of the canon allows any baptized person who receives "the laying on of hands by a Bishop of this Church at Confirmation or Reception" to be considered as both baptized and confirmed. But the canon does not identify who is to be confirmed and who is to be received. Any baptized person, from any church, could be received with the laying on of hands. The canon does not limit reception to those in churches with the historic episcopate, although it requires laying on of hands, which is not specified in the rubrics for the rite.

The 1997 General Convention attempted to clarify the matter by amending the canon to permit anyone who has previously made a mature public commitment in another church to be received rather than confirmed, and the 2003 Convention further amended the canon to stipulate the laying on of hands by a bishop of the Episcopal Church. Presumably this would include, for example, a Methodist baptized as an infant and confirmed in early adolescence, a Baptist baptized as a teenager, or a Roman Catholic initiated as an adult in a rite that included confirmation by the parish priest. The multiple revisions of the canon reflect the divergence of interpretation as well as an ecumenical sensitivity.

The 2003 General Convention also adopted a resolution to clarify processes for incorporating members in light of the relationship of full communion begun with the Evangelical Lutheran Church in America (ELCA) on January 1, 2001. The resolution stated that the prayer book and the canons allow members of the ELCA to be received. Subsequently, the Office of Ecumenical and Interfaith Relations issued guidelines explaining that members of the ELCA may be transferred into Episcopal congregations, following the canon that details the process for communicants to be transferred into another congregation. The practices reported by bishops in 2005, however, indicate that many continued to receive or confirm Lutherans.

Such attempts to determine the equivalent of Confirmation could be set aside were we to relinquish our insistence on confirmation as a requirement for leadership positions in the Episcopal Church. We would then be free to respond pastorally to those who come to the Episcopal Church after baptized membership in another branch of Christ's church.

Consider, for example, Jane, a mature Christian woman who was baptized as an infant and raised in an Eastern Orthodox Church. As an adult, she found her way to the Episcopal Church, the worship resonating with her liturgical formation in Eastern Orthodoxy, the support for women's ministries affirming her experience as a woman. Jane became an active member of her congregation, worshiping every Sunday, singing in the choir, participating in a women's Bible study, providing leadership for outreach projects. She considers herself fully a member of the Episcopal Church, though she has never been formally received or confirmed. The catholicity of the Episcopal Church is particularly appealing to Jane, that is that we recognize her as a member because she has been baptized with water in the triune name and added to the parish membership rolls. Jane is well suited to serve on a Vestry or as a lay Eucharistic minister or a member of a churchwide commission. To insist on a ritual equivalent of Confirmation would diminish the significance of Jane's baptism—after all, we proclaim one Lord, one faith, one baptism, one God and Father of all. Requiring confirmation in some form would also minimize Jane's formation in the Episcopal Church through regular participation in its worship and ministry.

I am not proposing that we ignore the unique contours of our Anglican heritage as we welcome Christians from other parts of the body of Christ. We ought to provide regular opportunities for study and reflection on the gifts and challenges that come with our Anglican way of following Christ, and we ought to offer such opportunity not only to those newly affiliating with the Episcopal Church but also to longtime, even lifelong members of the Episcopal Church.

Nor am I proposing that we abandon altogether the option for a ritual form of reception into the Episcopal Church. Susan's story, for example, is rather different from that of Jane. Susan was raised in the Roman Catholic Church, baptized as an infant, making her first communion at age seven and then confirmed at age ten. She discovered particular gifts for music and found that the church welcomed those gifts. Eventually Susan joined the staff of a local Roman Catholic parish, her sense of call to ministry growing through her service as minister of music. She went to seminary, earning first a master's degree and then entering an ecumenical Doctor of Ministry program. Continuing to ponder her vocation, she began to perceive a call to ordination. A mentor nudged Susan toward the Episcopal Church, and after considerable prayer, she and her family began worshiping in a nearby congregation. Eventually, Susan and her family were presented to the bishop and received. For Susan, this ritual expression of her welcome into the Episcopal Church was powerful, a sense of coming home, an acceptance for which she had been hungering for years. Continuing in the ordination process would require some ritual equivalent of confirmation, but this was not Susan's primary motive for being received by the bishop.

For Susan and for others, a ritual expression of their decision to join the Episcopal Church is a profound statement of belonging, marking a significant transition in their journey of faith. Offering a rite of reception into the Episcopal Church is an important pastoral gesture, even if it is not to be required for membership or for service or leadership in the Church.

In contrast to Susan's experience, Sam did not find his ritual reception into the Episcopal Church to be deeply meaningful. Like Susan, he was raised in the Roman Catholic Church and served as a lay minister for many years. He found his way to the Episcopal Church, became active in his local congregation, and eventually began to discern a call to ordination. Although confirmed in the Roman Catholic Church, he had not been received by a bishop of the Episcopal Church. The bishop's next visit to Sam's parish was months away, and the requirement that he be canonically "baptized and confirmed" in the Episcopal Church was preventing him from taking the next step in the ordination process. So he was sent off to a neighboring parish, where the bishop was visiting, to be formally received. For Sam, his reception was little more than a perfunctory jump through a hoop. I suspect that even if he had waited for the bishop to visit his home parish, his reception would not have altered his perception of his membership in the Episcopal Church, much less marked a significant transition in his life.

Jane, Susan, Sam, and others affiliating with the Episcopal Church would be better served by a rite of reception administered by a priest in their new congregation, welcoming them into the Episcopal Church and acknowledging their new membership. These new members could eventually reaffirm their faith in the presence of a bishop, whether in a congregational affirmation of the Baptismal Covenant during the bishop's visit or through the rite of reaffirmation.

RE-IMAGINING CONFIRMATION

Twentieth century theologians have called Confirmation a rite in search of a theology. Given the grab-bag of meanings and practices that have developed over the course of many centuries, it is not surprising that the Episcopal Church continues to wrestle with the interpretation and implementation of the 1979 rite and the canons subsequently adopted. There remains passionate support in the Episcopal Church for a rite of public affirmation of faith that includes the laying on of hands by a bishop, even as others give little attention to Confirmation and related rites.

Imagine that Confirmation, Reception, and Reaffirmation are offered as pastoral responses to significant turning points in Christian life. Getting clarity about these rites of renewal will enable us to live more fully into the understanding of baptism as "full initiation by water and the Holy Spirit into Christ's Body the Church." In the waters of baptism, every Christian is born to new life in Christ and empowered for Christian ministry and discipleship. Confirmation and related rites of affirmation can be effective ritual expressions of renewed and deepened commitment, although they are not essential for Christian faith and life.

Confirmation is especially appropriate for those baptized as infants or young children. Although they participate in the regular renewal of baptism through the Eucharist and through the Renewal of Baptismal Vows at the Easter Vigil and other baptismal feasts, they can benefit by making a personal affirmation of faith and commitment to the responsibilities of baptism that others undertook on their behalf. This opportunity is not, however, a new commissioning for ministry or admission to some new status of membership. Already ministers by virtue of their baptism, preparation for Confirmation is an opportunity for them to reflect on their gifts for ministry, the ways they have already been engaged in ministry in the world and in the Church, and the ways they might minister in the future. Their preparation, part of a lifelong process of formation, is also a time to explore their faith and the challenges of Christian discipleship today. At the conclusion of their preparation, they make a mature decision about whether they are ready to be confirmed.

A rite of reception for those affiliating with the Episcopal Church is also pastorally desirable. Imagine a rite for any baptized person becoming a member of a particular congregation in the Episcopal Church. Preparation for this rite introduces new members to the practices of the congregation, for example its outreach ministries and its educational offerings for children and adults. For those new to the Episcopal Church, preparation includes information about the history, structure, and governance of the Episcopal Church and Anglican Communion. Those who are already Episcopalians contribute their experiences of the Church. At the congregation's regular Sunday Eucharist, the new members are presented by name and promise to join the community in living into their baptism, members of the assembly pledge their support, a prayer of blessing is offered for the new members, and they write their names into the church's register of baptized members. By adding their names to the register, all are now members of the Episcopal Church. Like other members of the church, these new members participate in the regular renewal of baptism through participation in the Eucharist and the periodic Renewal of Baptismal Vows, and they are eligible to hold office and serve in lay liturgical ministries. For some this is sufficient, while others of these new Episcopalians, like Susan, will desire a more formal, ritual association with the bishop. Those in the latter group are later presented, whether on the occasion of a bishop's visit to the congregation or as part of a diocesan confirmation service, and received with the laying on of hands by the bishop.

Those baptized as adults or older children, whether by a priest or bishop, make a personal affirmation of faith and commitment to baptismal living at their baptism. Their preparation helps shape their discipleship through reflection on scripture, prayer, worship, and their gifts for ministry. No additional rite is required; they are fully initiated and eligible to hold office and serve in licensed ministries in the Episcopal Church. At a later time, after experiencing a renewal or deepening of faith, they may reaffirm that faith in the presence of a bishop. However, not all who are baptized as adults will participate in this rite. For them, regular participation in worship is sufficient to reaffirm their faith and renew their commitment to Christian discipleship.

By offering people the opportunity to affirm their faith and receive laying on of hands by their bishop, rather than requiring confirmation or its equivalent for holding office in the Church, the Episcopal Church can more fully embrace its teaching that baptism is full initiation into the Church. People are more likely to receive the rite gratefully, as a pastoral response to their growth in faith, rather than as a hoop they must jump through in order to serve in the Church. Those who hold office in the Church must be instructed in its history, structure, and governance, in order to serve effectively. Accountability for receiving such instruction could be managed in a manner similar to requirements for training in the prevention of sexual abuse and misconduct. An ongoing pattern of faithful Christian living is also essential for Church leaders. The canonical standard for a communicant in good standing—one who is "faithful in corporate worship" and "faithful in working, praying, and giving for the spread of the Kingdom of God"—provides a sufficient standard by which to determine eligibility for leadership, lay or ordained.

Developing a more coherent practice of Confirmation, Reception, and Reaffirmation and clarifying expectations for those holding office in the Church will also make administration of the rite just one expression of the bishop's overall ministry as chief pastor and teacher, one who baptizes and encourages all the baptized to utilize their gifts for ministry to the fullest extent possible. Confirmation, Reception, and Reaffirmation will then be part of lifelong Christian formation, opportunities for personal renewal and reaffirmation complementing the periodic renewal of baptismal vows at the Easter Vigil and other baptismal feasts and in the weekly celebration of the Eucharist.

• • •

Ruth A. Meyers is Hodges-Haynes Professor of Liturgics and Dean of Academic Affairs at Church Divinity School of the Pacific in Berkeley, California. Author of *Continuing the Reformation: Re-Visioning Baptism in the Episcopal Church* (Church Publishing, 1997), she is completing work on a book on missional worship (forthcoming from Eerdmans). She is the current chair of the Standing Commission on Liturgy and Music and has been a Deputy to four General Conventions. She is a member of the Council of Associated Parishes for Liturgy and Mission and has been a participant in the International Anglican Liturgical Consultation since 1991.

CHAPTER 6

A Liturgy for the Messy Middle

James R. Mathes

I remember the day my thinking shifted about confirmation. It was my second regular visitation to St. Dunstan's in the San Carlos neighborhood of east San Diego. I had met Martin and his mother on my previous visitation to the parish. Martin's mental retardation was immediately evident. When the rector took me in to meet the confirmation group for this visit, I was surprised to see that Martin was there with his mother. I think the rector picked up on my reaction to Martin's anticipated confirmation. As we prepared for the service, he made a point of telling me about all the work he had done with Martin and that he felt it was time for his confirmation. I was not convinced. And in my relatively brief conversations with Martin and the other confirmands, I did not have a chance to discern his understanding of the faith. In the rush of the morning, I simply had to trust the rector.

The service began and all went well until the moment Martin came forward so that I could lay hands on his head and say the confirmation prayer over him. Who knows why he got scared, but he did. He began to wail and recoil. Maybe the miter and crozier in procession had made him understandably wary of me. Those who had gone before him seemed no worse for the experience. But he was having none of this business and did not want to come up the chancel steps. As his mother and sponsors tried to coax him forward, he became increasingly loud and agitated. In a moment that I can only attribute to the Spirit, I started to walk down to Martin. With one hand I reassured him with a pat on the shoulder; he looked at me and smiled. I asked if I could pray for him and he nodded his assent. I placed my other hand on his head and prayed the confirmation prayer, "Defend, O Lord, your servant Martin, with your heavenly grace, that he may continue yours forever, and daily increase in your Holy Spirit more and more, until he comes to your everlasting kingdom."

Martin's "Amen" was a big smile and a hug for his bishop. I do not know all that the Holy Spirit did to Martin behind the veil of his mental handicaps. What I do know is that something happened. That moment was incredibly powerful for me, for Martin, and the congregation.

Before my experience with Martin, I was somewhat confused about confirmation. All too often I found that those being confirmed did not take it seriously. It was the young adult version of "getting the baby done." Too often it felt like a shame. As a response, I found myself oscillating between thinking that it was indeed an exit rite whose time had passed, or one that needed to be guarded by high ecclesial expectations. Martin changed all that. Or perhaps, it is more accurate to say that Martin's confirmation began a process of discernment that has led me to see what we do in baptism, formation, and confirmation in a substantially different way.

BEGINNINGS AND ENDINGS

So much of the energy of human existence goes into beginnings and endings. We remember beginnings religiously: birthdays and anniversaries come to mind. Graduations, assuredly an ending, are called commencements. Indeed, a survey of the Book of Common Prayer shows that our communal life is significantly focused on beginnings and endings. Our daily office is dominated by morning and evening prayer—that which begins and ends each day. Baptism, marriage, burial, and ordination are all about beginnings and endings. However, the prayer book gives very little attention to what happens in life between the beginning of things and the end. Confirmation stands out in the life of the Christian community as an exception. There is also Reconciliation of a Penitent and the Ministration to the Sick, but both of these are essentially private moments. What we celebrate in community are beginnings and endings except for this thing called confirmation.

The Eucharistic prayers are literally and figuratively in the middle of the prayer book. They can be seen to be liturgies for the middle. However, Eucharist is altogether a different kind of liturgy. Theologically, it is both within time and beyond, celebrated at a table, which is at once in heaven and on earth. And Eucharist interconnects with everything. It is a part of every beginning, every baptism, ordination, or marriage, and every ending, every burial. Eucharist is the sacrament of unity on the journey of discipleship best summarized in the memorial acclamation of Jesus' journey: Christ has died. Christ has risen. Christ will come again. We celebrate the Eucharist to make his journey our journey. Eucharist is the constant, which means that what happens between noted beginnings and endings is less attended.

In her book, *Still: Notes on a Mid-Faith Crisis*, Lauren F. Winner defines the middle as fertile spiritual territory. Having gone through two crises, the death of her mother and a divorce, she thoughtfully allows the reader to inhabit a spiritual wilderness of doubting and rearranging her relationship with God. I remember a colleague who once wisely said that people have two predictable ways of handling the discomfort of grief and change: denial or rushing through. Winner, instead of either less-than-healthy response, reflects and blesses the time after her loss. In so doing, she calls attention to the middle times of our spiritual journeys.

In one of her reflections, she ponders a painting by Fitz Lane, "The Western Shore with Norman's Woe." Like so many works of art, she points out that it is the middle tones, the greys, browns, and blues, that give the painting depth and power. Springing from this image, she writes:

> Perhaps middle tint is the palette of faithfulness. Middle tint is going to church each week, opening the prayer book each day. This is rote, unshowy behavior, and you would not notice it if you weren't looking for it, but it is necessary; it is most of the canvas; it is the palette that makes possible the gashes of white, the outlines of black; it is indeed that by which the painting will succeed or fail.[1]

Winner is onto something that may have important implications for how we perform our sacraments as a church and how those sacramental moments fit into the warp and weft of the spiritual life.

THE SPIRITUAL MIDDLE

For several years, I worked in boarding schools, part of that time teaching mathematics to middle schoolers. One of my colleagues said more than once that middle-schoolers were like piranha: one of them was kinda cute, but a school of them could eat you alive! The image may translate to the

---

1. Lauren F. Winner, *Still: Notes on a Mid-Faith Crisis* (San Franciso: HarperOne, 2013), 190.

church and congregation. For we are all in the middle. We are all in the midst of growing up, being formed, living into our baptismal faith—the list goes on. And being in the middle is simply messy.

There is very little commonality in the middle. We grow at different rates. We come with different skills and abilities. As Paul says, "Now there are varieties of gifts, but the same Spirit; and there are varieties of services, but the same Lord; and there are varieties of activities, but it is the same God who activates all of them in everyone."[2] The middle bears out the quintessential challenge of unity and diversity. We are bound together and yet we are so different. An analogy is a race. The starting line is the same. The finish line is the same. But in the middle, every runner has a different stride and pace. Some are better at hills than others. A few will simply have to walk part of the way. The middle is where each runs his or her own race. And yet all will cover the same distance. All are in it together. While each has a private struggle, together the runners will celebrate the finish line.

In the ancient church, there was a vital sense of the Christian life with a beginning, middle, and end. The middle was very much the main thing. After all, the earliest Christians were simply said to be people of "The Way." Race, journey, the Way: the life of discipleship in Jesus Christ was a movement. The beginning was a clear beginning in baptism with intentional communal travel—the middle. And the end, whether through martyrdom or a quiet death, was also a beginning of life eternal.

With Constantine and the institutional church, pervasive social structures took over the middle ground. The Way was not unique, but ubiquitous. It was not the way, but the norm to claim Christian identity. Over time, that identity was neither striking nor costly. It simply was.

In the United States of the last century, when the Episcopal Church evolved much of its present structure, presuppositions, and mores, our church could assume a certain Christianization as a byproduct simply of education and social interaction. The church could assume that people understood the basic contours of the Christian life. Literature and scripture commingled. Education and Christian formation overlapped. The patterns of social life and liturgical life were in sync.

That was the world, still, of the first half of the last century to which we are heirs. It is the church that, to some extent, we still inhabit—a church that serves the world as a station to which people come for baptism,

---

2. 1 Corinthians 12:4–6.

marriage, and funerals—or as has been suggested: hatch, match, and dis-
patch. That church did not need to focus on the middle because the middle was covered by the academy and the family structure.

Now, family structures have changed dramatically. The academy is
completely secular in orientation. Over time, the institutional church has
become increasingly untethered from the world around it. No wonder
people talk about being spiritual but not religious.

In the midst of this tectonic shift, the Episcopal Church went
through the process of prayer book revision. The liturgical luminaries of
that movement guided our church to reclaim much of our liturgical heritage of the first centuries, a decidedly missionary time in the history of
the church. Baptism is recovered as a communal event and the true anchor
to the beginning of the life of discipleship. The Eucharist is the center
of that community life, in which we relentlessly come to the table of the
Lord to remember his life, death, resurrection, and promise to come again.
It orients the faith community to the horizon—the end.

Those familiar with the process of creating the present prayer book
will know that leaders of prayer book revision had hoped for a much more
dramatic change in so-called rites of initiation. Returning to the ancient
pattern of the early church, the liturgical luminaries of prayer book revision advocated, in the words of the preface to *Prayer Book Studies 18*, for:

> . . . the reunion of Baptism, Confirmation, and Communion into a
> single continuous service, as it was in the primitive Church. Thus, the
> entire liturgy will be recognized as the full reception of the candidate
> into the family of God by the power of the Holy Spirit: beginning with
> the acceptance through faith, of forgiveness of sins and redemption in
> Christ—of burial with Christ in the water in order that we may rise
> in him to newness of life; followed by the conferring of the gifts of the
> Spirit by the Laying on of hands; and ending with participation in the
> holy meal at which the entire family is united, nourished, and sanctified.[3]

Faced with resistance, principally from bishops purportedly concerned
with their episcopal prerogatives, the present prayer book is a compro-
mise with a robust baptismal service and a confirmation service as a later,
strongly encouraged act.

---

3. *Prayer Book Studies 18*, 19.

There are some today that argue that the time has come to complete the unfinished work of prayer book revision. These wise and thoughtful scholars suggest that Confirmation is a "rite in search of meaning" and that it continues to be confused as a "completing" baptism. They are particularly concerned about the instructions found before the confirmation service:

> In the course of their Christian development, those baptized at an early age are expected, when they are ready and have been duly prepared, to make a mature public affirmation of their faith and commitment to the responsibilities of their Baptism and to receive the laying on of hands by the bishop.[4]

This rubric injunction and canonical requirements make it clear that there is still an expectation of confirmation as a normative moment in one's faith formation. In this post-modern, post-Christian world, the question is, are we now in a post-confirmation church? Remembering the wisdom that we either deny or rush through transitions, it seems that we are doing both. Those who think we can hold fast to yesteryear and Confirmation as a sort of adolescent rite of passage are in denial. Those who think we should simply rush it to a quick and ready grave are in danger of disposing of something of immense value. For Confirmation can and should be the sacramental rite for the middle.

CONFIRMATION AS THE MIDDLE SACRAMENT

As a people who live our theology through prayer, we should look at what precisely we say when we confirm. The two prayers at the time of the laying on of hands by the bishop should be our principal texts:

> Strengthen, O Lord, your servant *N.* with your Holy Spirit; empower *him* for your service; and sustain *him* all the days of *his* life. *Amen.*

> Defend, O Lord, your servant *N.* with your heavenly grace, that *he* may continue yours for ever, and daily increase in your Holy Spirit more and more, until *he* comes to your everlasting kingdom. *Amen.*[5]

---

4. BCP 412.

5. BCP 418.

First of all, there is nothing in either of these prayers or in the words that precede or follow that suggest either explicitly or implicitly that baptism will not be fully baptism without this action. Indeed, the baptismal promises have just been renewed by all present: the bishop, any clergy, all who are present, including the candidates for confirmation.

Rather, these prayers seem most apt for someone in the middle of his or her faith journey. They are prayers for initial moments of renewal and recognition of spiritual maturity for those on The Way—living into the discipleship of Jesus Christ. In the first, we pray that the person be strengthened, empowered for service, and sustained. In the second, that God defend her, that she continues to be counted as God's and that she increases in the Holy Spirit more and more. These prayers are for growth in the spirit at this time—this middle time. They are not done yet but they are on The Way.

However, for Confirmation to truly be the sacramental rite for the middle, it will have to continue to change in more specific and intentional ways. Martin gave me the first, and perhaps most important, glimpse into what needs to change.

When I was confirmed in 1971 using the 1928 Book of Common Prayer, like so many before me and at that time, Confirmation was an adolescent rite of passage which included a great deal of rote memorization—the Apostle's Creed, the General Thanksgiving, the Prayer of Humble Access, the Nicene Creed, to name a few. Before Confirmation, I came to the altar rail for a blessing; after Confirmation, I received communion. It was made very clear to me that now I was an adult in the church.

Even though we have changed our practices around communion, we still have vestiges of Confirmation as a rite of passage for adolescents. Curricula abound that are designed to move adolescents through this transition punctuated by the bishop's visitation. Learn this, believe this, receive Confirmation. That is the real message.

Martin upsets this linear progression. He could not learn as I once did. Whatever he believed was his and was not easily shared. When the institution incarnated in this bishop stood before him to lay upon him Confirmation, he recoiled. The gift of the Holy Spirit to me in that moment was a reflex of adaptation. I left the symbols of office behind and went to Martin. I asked him if he wanted me to pray over him. The laying on of hands was not his Confirmation; it was the hug.

Confirmation in the twenty-first century is going to need to change. It may no longer even be appropriate to call it Confirmation. In this time, such a rite will need to be adaptive. It will need to be a rite that can join people in The Way to strengthen and empower them for service. Like all middles, this middle is messy. As an adaptive time in the life of the Church, we should use the present rite of Confirmation in a creative way to serve people who have reached seminal points in the faith journey. It is a rite for the epiphany events. It is a rite for the turns in the road—the *metanoia* moments. Certainly in this adaptive time, some will find this moment in their adolescence, but more often than not, it will come at an unexpected time. Formation in this adaptive time will need to be less programmatic and more organic, action oriented, and community based. It will be formation that connects the dots between the liturgy and lectionary, the events of daily life and the hopes and hurts of the world. It will put the church, including those in early formation, in vulnerable places— thin places—where they serve those most vulnerable and in so doing are gifted to be Jesus for today's world. It is conversion from the outside in rather than from the inside out. I think of our new Episcopal Church Center in San Diego where more than hundreds, mostly homeless, poor, and unemployed, are served every month either by receiving hot meals, stocking their cupboards from our food pantry, receiving care at the medical clinic, or even getting a haircut. In this same place, the new diocesan School for Ministry meets every Saturday and our diocesan staff carries out the work of diocesan administration. From this experiment in mission, the word and example is spreading as our congregations learn how to be the servant church in their particular place. As followers of Jesus, we learn by doing and what we are doing is being Jesus for the world.

This is the church in the middle. And because we are a church that prays our theology, we need to have a rite for this middle time. Confirmation is that rite in this adaptive time. If in the not too distant future the Episcopal Church considers prayer revision, we should preserve a rite for the middle that serves as a moment of prayer for strengthening and empowerment for the life of faith. At the very least it should have these attributes:

- A different title for the rite: by changing the name, the church can break with the more problematic presupposition—the baggage of confirmation. Building on the service form found in the Book of Common Prayer following the Confirmation service, such a rite could be called, "A Service of Christian Commitment." Or it could be more daringly called, "A Service of Renewal on The Way."

- The service should be renewable: this issue was hotly debated in the previous prayer book revision, which resulted in the reaffirmation option in our current service. The theology of the present Confirmation does not preclude doing the act again. Indeed, the middle of the Christian life is long and messy. There may be several moments of renewal.

- The bishop should be the celebrant: there are other denominations where local ministers confirm. However, in our tradition, the bishop is the church's symbol of unity. For the bishop to act in this moment is to create that outward and visible sign of unity at the junction of missional intention.

- Conserve what gives meaning: the manual action of the laying on of hands and the prayers currently used should be retained. In the midst of change, this will create continuity with the past. As already suggested, the prayers speak the very theology needed for the moment of renewal.

By being attentive to the middle of the spiritual life, we have a chance to change the sacramental rite of Confirmation in such a way that it will nurture, strengthen, empower, and renew disciples in the midst of their spiritual lives. Martin taught me that even the most unconventional liturgical moment could do just that. His enduring gift to me is to trust that God will act even and especially when we least expect it. While liturgy is the work of the people, it is also the place where the Holy Spirit surprises.

About a year after Martin's confirmation, he was tragically killed in a car accident. Had he lived to be present at my next visitation, I wonder if he would have asked me to confirm him again. If he had, I hope I would have done just that. You probably have seen the bumper sticker that those who adopt rescue dogs often have with the question: who rescued who? At Martin's confirmation, I asked a similar question: who confirmed who? The Church, all Jesus' followers, need more moments like that! May that be our passion and our longing.

· · ·

The Right Reverend James R. Mathes is the fourth bishop of the Diocese of San Diego. He began his career as an educator at St. Andrew's-Sewanee, an Episcopal school in Tennessee. As a priest in the Diocese of Massachusetts, he designed a high school confirmation curriculum that included surveys of other religions and culminated with the learner presenting their own creedal statement. As canon to the ordinary, he brought mentoring opportunities to new clergy in the Diocese of Chicago with a $1.6 million grant from the Lilly Endowment.

CHAPTER 7

A Rite in Search
for a Reason of Being

Lee Alison Crawford

CONTEXTUAL CONSIDERATIONS

In twenty years of parish ministry, almost all served in Vermont, I have baptized far more people, young and old, and presented slightly more people for reception into the church than I have presented for confirmation. My comments, therefore, draw heavily on a particular context: the small, family-size congregation in a rural diocese with only two "metropolitan" areas, a few small cities, and not many true suburbs. The three congregations I have served in Vermont have a disproportionate amount of people over forty and only a handful of children and youth. Context means so much.

Regardless the size of congregation, Episcopalians still struggle with a continued confusion about the function of Confirmation and its place in the life of the Church. Are people confirmed because it is the expected norm for a contributing member of society? Does Confirmation meet a pastoral need? Does the Church use Confirmation as a measuring stick for determining membership? Or, does Confirmation fulfill all of the above considerations? What, exactly, does Confirmation mean in the Episcopal Church of today?

As a way of moving from these theoretical questions about Confirmation, this essay begins with some flesh-and-blood examples. Readers might find familiar some of these vignettes related to Confirmation from the past fifty years in the Episcopal Church:

- 1958: A young father decides to get confirmed, not because he believes in God or attends church, but because it is the socially proper thing to do and a sign of support for his wife, whom he has charged with raising their children in the Christian faith—should she wish to do so. The children do not even know their father was confirmed until they run across an inscribed 1928 Book of Common Prayer on a top shelf in his office years later.

- 1968: In a suburban congregation, a class of middle school students (mostly sixth and seventh graders) meets with an earnest rector responsible for their preparation for this rite of passage. Most of the kids in the class do their utmost to annoy the priest, but others try to pay attention because they know they have to take a mid-term and final exam before the great day arrives when they will stand in front of the bishop. Confirmation class meets once a week for ninety minutes for seven months. This writer only remembers the admonishment to know how to spell properly "Episcopalian," "Epiphany," and "Quinquagesima." She yearns to receive Holy Communion, which has been denied her because she is not confirmed. At the same time, during her confirmation class, she realizes that she desires to be a priest someday even though women's ordination still is not a possibility—why, she cannot even serve as acolyte; only her brother can because he is a boy.

- 1985: A woman asks her parish priest, "Whatever happened to Confirmation? How come children now can receive communion? When I was growing up, we had to wait until we were confirmed to have communion."

- 1996: The bishop makes her visitation to a congregation. Much to the priest's surprise, after communion and before the final blessing, the bishop issues an "altar call," inviting any and all to come forward for the laying on of hands and a blessing. As the priest watches the entire congregation come forward—elders in their 90s and parents bringing forward their infant children—she wonders how long it has been, particularly for the elders, since a bishop's hands have touched their heads. By the time the altar call is over, half the congregation is in tears with wonder at this connection with the Holy Spirit and pastoral gesture of the bishop. Though what the bishop performed is not Confirmation, the priest wonders how parishioners interpreted her pastoral gesture.

- 1998: A fourteen-year-old has never been baptized. After his grandmother's death, his parents and he begin to attend the local congregation. The fourteen-year-old desires baptism, so the priest suggests that the bishop baptize him during his visitation. After he has marked the young man's forehead with the oil of chrismation, the bishop whispers to him, "You don't need to be confirmed now."

- 2001: In response to the events of 9/11, a ninth-grader feels something is missing in her life. Even though she was baptized as an infant, the family's church attendance has been sporadic. Post 9/11, she attends almost weekly, and when the rector announces confirmation classes, she signs up on her own. Her older sibling looks on with a certain element of longing as his younger sister goes through a rite that he had not known was possible for him. Years later, neither attends church.

- 2005: One evening at a vestry meeting, the rector mentions in passing that in order to serve on the vestry, a person must be a communicant in good standing, confirmed, and "on the books." She is operating from the parish bylaws, which have not caught up with the Constitution and Canons, as well as the memory that when she first was ordained one had to be confirmed to be on the vestry. She does not recognize her error. The next day, she receives a frantic call from the junior warden, who wants to meet with her immediately. In their face-to-face meeting, the junior warden tearfully tells the rector that he has never been confirmed; he grew up in the United Church of Christ, and therefore he will need to resign. The rector replies that even though it goes against the bylaws, she will not accept the junior warden's resignation, because of all the people on the vestry he is the most faithful in attending church, wrestling with questions of faith, and living out in daily life the baptismal vows he made and reaffirms. She tells him, "In a small congregation I would say Confirmation is an ideal for leadership, but in practice it is not essential."

- 2010: The priest-in-partnership announces that the bishop will be coming for his annual visitation six months off, and those desiring Confirmation, Reception, or Reaffirmation of Baptismal Vows should speak with the priest. He also specifically asks all the high school youth who attend church if they would like to be confirmed. To a person, they turn him down, saying they do not think they want to get confirmed. Meanwhile, parents of sixth and seventh graders approach the priest-in-partnership, asking him why he is not inviting their children for Confirmation. When the bishop arrives for his visitation, he confirms one person and receives two others—all adults.

As a caveat, all but one of these examples took place in New England and several in Vermont, the least "churched" state and second smallest state in the United States. Context weighs heavily on the understanding and practice of confirmation. According to parochial reports submitted to the Episcopal Church and tallied by Dr. Kirk Hadaway, 2011 total confirmations for Province I, New England (seven dioceses with 615 congregations and 189,187 active members), were 931 children and 583 adults.[1] For my small diocese, Vermont, the figures were 14 youth and 29 adult confirmations, the lowest in the province. These numbers, as with any set of numbers, need qualification—namely, the bishop does not visit all the congregations in a single year but rather completes a cycle every eighteen months.[2]

By contrast, it is not unusual for the bishop diocesan, the Right Reverend Jean Zaché Duracin, of the Episcopal Church of Haiti, the Episcopal Church's largest diocese, to confirm hundreds at one visitation. The Reverend Fedner Esaie Dorceus, priest of that church, wrote the author that, "In the zone of the Central Plateau in one visitation, it [the number of confirmands] can be more than two hundred. The [total] number of confirmations is 1,000 to 1,265 for a year."[3] Though no longer part of TEC as of 1998, the Episcopal Anglican Diocese of El Salvador, now member of the Anglican Church of the Region of Central America, demonstrates how context further affects the rite. There, the bishop, the Right Reverend Martín Barahona, on an average confirms fifty people (breakdown of youth and adults not available) but receives over two hundred people a year.[4] Most Salvadoran Episcopalians are converts from the Roman Catholic Church— hence, the much higher figure for reception.

---

1. *http://www.episcopalchurch.org/sites/default/files/2011_table_of_statistics_of_the_episcopal_church.pdf*

2. Elizabeth Allison, Historian for the Diocese of Vermont, noted in a September 12, 2013 email: "This is raw data compiled from the Bishop's Reports of Official Acts from the Convention Journals with no identification of the Congregations visited . . . Because of the many variables involved, it is impossible to draw any valid conclusions such as the name and size of the congregation visited, that Bishop [Thomas Ely] does not visit every congregation each year; that congregations can have a 'banner year' because of a new rector, etc."

3. "Dans la zone du plateau central dans une année ça peut être plus que 200, le nombre est 1000 à 1265 pour une année," personal correspondance, September 7, 2013. C.f., *http://www.episcopal church.org/sites/default/files/2011_table_of_statistics_of_the_episcopal_church.pdf*. Officially, the figure for 2011 was 557 children and 647 adults in Haiti. For the same year: c.f. Honduras, 126 and 90. In Honduras, 25 people were received, whereas in Haiti 156 people were received. Note that in 2011, the membership for the Episcopal Church of Haiti was 86,424 in 100 congregations; Honduras has 134 congregations with a membership of 49,913.

4. "El Obispo me ha comentado tambien que celebra un promedio de 50 confirmaciones por año y 200 recibimientos." Personal correspondance with the Executive Administrator, Ana Miriam Romero, September 12, 2013.

THEOLOGICAL CONSIDERATIONS

Even four decades into use of the 1979 prayer book, we as a Church still struggle with understanding what exactly Confirmation means and how to articulate clearly a theology of this misunderstood rite. Leonel Mitchell stated that, "Confirmation is one of the problems left unresolved in the Book of Common Prayer 1979."[5] He suggests we should go as far as to avoid using the word "confirmation" altogether, "since its meaning is almost always ambiguous."[6]

The Episcopal Church entered into this period of confusion after the 1970 General Convention had authorized admission of children to communion before Confirmation, hitherto considered the dividing line between baptism and full initiation into the life of the Church. Subsequent conventions struggled to clarify the role of Confirmation vis-á-vis baptism, now considered—at least ideally if not in practice—a complete rite of initiation. Yet there remains that one line inserted into the rubrics of the 1979 Prayer Book: "Those baptized as adults, unless baptized with the laying on of hands by a bishop, are also expected to make a public affirmation of their faith and commitment to the responsibilities of their Baptism in the presence of a bishop and to receive the laying on of hands,"[7] which calls into question the supremacy of baptism. The Reverend Dr. Ruth Meyers observes: "This rubric, added at the eleventh hour at the General Convention when the proposed Book of Common Prayer was presented for approval, suggests that baptism is not full Christian initiation unless an individual receives the imposition of hands by a bishop."[8]

Yet the 1979 Book of Common Prayer assumes baptism as its root metaphor. It even states, "Holy Baptism is full initiation by water and the Holy Spirit into Christ's Body the Church."[9] The Great Vigil of Easter, which segues into the baptismal rite, lies at the heart of the Prayer Book, with the rest of the Prayer Book radiating outward—the Christian year, special rites (Holy Week), the collects and the Daily Office in one direction, and the Holy Eucharist, pastoral offices, and episcopal offices

---

5. Leonel Mitchell, "What Shall We Do About Confirmation?" in Ruth A. Meyers, ed., *A Prayer Book for the 21st Century, Prayer Book Studies 3* (New York: The Church Hymnal Corporation, 1996), 104.

6. Mitchell, in Meyers, ed., *Prayer Book Studies 3*, 107.

7. BCP 412.

8. Ruth Meyers, "Rites of Initiation," in Charles Hefling and Cynthia Shattuck, eds., *The Oxford Guide to the Book of Common Prayer: A Worldwide Survey* (Oxford, NY: Oxford University Press, 2006), 489.

9. BCP 298.

in the other direction (the psalter, supplemental collects, historical documents, tables for the year, and lectionaries stand on their own). While it is true that Confirmation appears both in the baptismal rite and in episcopal offices, it does not occupy as significant a place in the structure of the Prayer Book as does baptism.

Even with our emphasis on baptism, muddled understandings abound. Whenever a person says that he or she was "baptized in the Episcopal Church," I gently add at an opportune time that they were baptized into "God's household";[10] it so happened that the baptism was celebrated in an Episcopal Church. That small reminder often surprises people until they pause and realize that, indeed, baptism does not speak of the Episcopal Church at all. (Nor does confirmation for that matter.)

The prayer book throughout presumes baptism to be the *sine qua non* for participation in the life of the church. When we consider the Catechism, we note that it speaks of the ministry of the laity, not the ministry of the baptized or confirmed (BCP 855). From all outward signs, baptism and solely baptism seems sufficient for full participation, inclusion, and membership in the life of the church.

BAPTISM AND CONFIRMATION IN PARISH LIFE

Given the lack of clarity about the place and theology of confirmation, it would seem that the church still subconsciously operates with sixteenth century theologian Martin Bucer's justification of confirmation as important because:

1. it would get the bishops out into the parishes;
2. examination in the catechism would be conducted by an outsider;
3. dignity or impressiveness would be added to the occasion;
4. this would be a sign of the catholicity of the church.[11]

How, then, do we handle the awkward place or lack of confirmation in quotidian parish life?

Returning to the examples at the head of this essay, one sees the variety of people's understandings of confirmation. The father gets confirmed

---

10. BCP 308.

11. Marion Hatchett, *Commentary on the American Prayer Book* (New York: Seabury Press, 1981), 260.

because it is the "civic" thing to do, i.e., that is what a "good" person did in a mainline Protestant church in the 1950s. Anthony Robinson characterizes this response as "a blend of good citizenship, middle-class morality, and golden-rule Christianity," which is not inherently bad but which "does not go far enough."[12] Fewer and fewer people today desire to be confirmed than fifty years ago for those reasons.

Moreover, there has been a movement away from confirming children as they enter middle school, rather waiting until they have navigated the vicissitudes of puberty. Wrangling a group of sixth graders into confirmation just because "that is what we have always done" does not allow for differing levels of maturity or desire (most important) to make this important commitment. A sixth grader may well have the desire and maturity, and in that case, of course, the child should be allowed to prepare for confirmation. Others simply are not ready and should not be pushed into confirmation.

Some clergy have tried innovative and, at times, questionable ways of inviting teens to go through confirmation class. A Lutheran pastor in Hanover, Germany, "issued confirmation cards entitling the parish's younger members to discounts in local shops. The Reverend Josef Kalkusch, a Lutheran pastor . . . has created a plastic card identifying teenagers enrolled in his church's confirmation class." His rationale was to create a loyalty club amidst the teens. In return, they are expected to engage in community service. Enticing teens to be consumers while preparing for confirmation seems contradictory.[13]

Not even ten years into living into the expression of baptism as the full initiation into the life of the church, thirty-six years ago in 1977 an Idaho priest "had suppressed a growing dissatisfaction with the traditional methods of preparing people for confirmation. . . . When Father Robert Noble finished his spring confirmation class in 1977, he drove home and told his wife, 'Never again. That's the last one I'll do.'" (How many parish priests, deacons, and lay educators share the same sentiment?) His solution was to create a weekend in which all ages gathered and people shared presentations and conversation on grace, prayer, the law, the Trinity, the work of Jesus Christ, sin and forgiveness, God's trust, the sacraments,

---

12. Anthony Robinson, *Changing the Conversation: A Third Way for Congregations* (Grand Rapids, MI: Wm. B. Eerdmans Publishing Co., 2008), 160. Note that these days, "membership" is less of a core value, whereas "discipleship" is; c.f., the discussion thereof in Robinson, 101–104.

13. *http://www.episcopalarchives.org/cgi-bin/ENS/ENSpress_release.pl?pr_number=2002-174-2*

the Church—the Body of Christ. Even in 1977, Noble expressed what more and more people think today: "The conventional confirmation class assumes that people already have a solid experience of Christianity. This isn't true today; in our post-Christian culture, faith and commitment cannot be assumed even in persons raised in Christian households, let alone those with no background in the Christian faith and life."[14]

PRACTICAL CONSIDERATIONS

Parish clergy today are confronted with the following expectations that often appear as conundrums:

- to reach out to people who have no church background, who are hesitant in joining "institutional religion," and who may or may not have been baptized (or may not know!);
- to foster a climate where baptism is understood as the primary entry point for all participation in the church;
- to respect the canons of the church where applicable;
- to provide for pastoral connections between a congregation and its bishop;
- to uphold one's responsibility of educating people about the Christian faith and life;
- and to present, when appropriate, candidates for confirmation and reception.[15]

I have focused less on the theology of confirmation than the pastoral practice of confirmation, because I see it as a marker in one's faith journey. Less essential is its standing as a sacrament. (Is it? Is it not?) When it comes to the pastoral practice regarding confirmation, I believe that some may avail themselves of the rite, but not all must. When the Holy Spirit invites a person to explore in more depth his or her faith, confirmation may or may not be the outcome. When it is the outcome, we rejoice in the

---

14. *http://www.episcopalarchives.org/cgi-bin/ENS/ENSpress_release.pl?pr_number=78247*

15. III.9.5.b.4: "It shall be the duty of Rectors or Priests-in-Charge to encourage and ensure the preparation of persons for Confirmation, Reception, and the Reaffirmation of Baptismal Vows, and to be ready to present them to the Bishop with a list of their names." Constitution and Canons 2012, General Convention Office (New York: Church Publishing, 2012), 98.

overt, conscious, and mature commitment of a Christian to his or her life in Christ.

Preparation for Confirmation (also reception and reaffirmation of one's baptismal vows) can enrich all who participate. Whether the preparation occurs during an intense weekend event or over a series of dinner conversations or "classes" after Sunday liturgy, the formation of a Christian community should be the end result. Two of the most meaningful confirmation preparations in which I have participated included a father-daughter who attended classes and were confirmed together—all the more poignant because the daughter died as a young adult—and then several years later, the afternoon conversations I had with two teenagers who wanted to get confirmed together. For the pastoral reasons enumerated, the preparation for Confirmation can provide a powerful means for strengthening community.

How do we reach out to those adults who spurned getting confirmed when the rest of their friends as teens were getting confirmed? One adult said he did not want to get confirmed as a teenager just so he could get his driver's license or be able to go out at night. He did not want to ascribe to something he wasn't sure he believed. Here, I believe that thoughtful discussions in a group of seekers or Episcopalians who desire a refresher course on the basic tenets of our faith and tradition can provide a safe locus for those adults who choose to enter more deeply into their life in Christ. Many times, also, a candidate's sponsors emerge from the class.

Understanding baptism as primary has influenced how I have approached parish ministry: the lack of being confirmed should not be an impediment to participation in the life and leadership of the congregation if a person otherwise participates regularly. Moreover, most positions of leadership nowadays do not require confirmation. In these circumstances, I err on the side of pastoral and contextual, rather than canonical, considerations. This choice does not assume, however, that just anybody will be invited to leadership positions: they must have demonstrated commitment to the breaking of the bread, the prayers and worship of the church, and show some awareness of who we are and what we believe as Episcopalians.

I agree with Leonel Mitchell who writes:

> I believe we should make it clear that those who personally make their own profession of faith at their baptism do not need to be confirmed. They have made their "mature public affirmation." This would eliminate

the theological nonsense of initiating an adult catechumen at the Easter vigil after an extensive period of preparation involving the whole congregation, and then "expecting" that this adult communicant will make a further profession of faith before a bishop three weeks later when episcopal visitation occurs.[16]

As I reflect on the example of the bishop issuing the altar call, I do believe there is an important connection created between a bishop, congregation, and candidates at the moment of confirmation. To see a bishop lay hands on those who have presented themselves for confirmation does underline the catholicity of the Church and our participation in the larger whole. To see candidates affirm—sometimes with tears— their commitment to journey with Christ reminds the rest of us of our connection to the Communion of Saints, that great cloud of witnesses. We can still find wisdom in the act of the laying on of hands; I do not believe that we should eliminate from our common worship that moment of connection, even if we do not fully understand or are unable to express a clear theology of confirmation. In this instance, the pastoral moment supersedes any explanation.

Ultimately, confirmation does become the locus of pastoral connection between priest, lay educators, mentors, candidate, and bishop. While its original and historic function may not apply today, confirmation is not a lost rite or one to be eliminated. In the life of a congregation, confirmation can well remind the whole body of the greater church of which it is a part and provide a moment for individuals to reaffirm their faith publically and commit themselves to living out this faith in the context of an Episcopal congregation.

• • •

The Reverend Canon Lee Alison Crawford, Ph.D., is a lifelong Episcopalian. She is Canon Missioner to the Episcopal Anglican Church of El Salvador, has worked with CREDO in Haiti, and is a six-time deputy to General Convention and former member of Executive Council. Most important, her heart lies with small congregations. Currently she is the Vicar of Church of Our Saviour in Killington, Vermont, a faith community with church, guesthouse, bakery, resident monastic, and 170 acres of land.

---

16. Mitchell, in Meyers, ed., *Prayer Book Studies 3*, 197.

CHAPTER 8

Contemplating Our
"One Wild and Precious Life"[1]

Victoria L. Garvey

S ome time ago when I was on the staff of a local congregation, I got a
call one morning from a woman I had never met. She said she'd heard
that we had a confirmation preparation program and that I was the one
organizing and teaching it. Both correct. And then she asked the question that many of us charged with such a ministry dread. "My daughter is
eleven and it's time to get her done; how do I sign her up?" Never mind
that I'd never heard of this woman or her daughter; never mind that they
had no connection with the congregation (membership and hospitality
are another issue best treated at another time). The woman, however well
intentioned, was betraying a bias from another age, an understanding of
the rite perhaps left over from her own childhood.

When I explained that her daughter might be a tad young for both
program and rite, she responded that her daughter was very bright and
knowledgeable for her age, advanced beyond her years. When I cited the
Book of Common Prayer with its caution that the rite is meant for those
who are ready to "make a mature affirmation of their faith and commitment to the responsibilities of their Baptism"[2] and that this meant, in part,
that such a step would have be her daughter's decision, she told me that
was ridiculous and that a child was not able to make that determination.
After that interesting declaration, she hung up on me.

Confirmation, confirmation, a wrench of contention in lots of theological and sacramental tool kits. Not that there's anything wrong with a
rite that re-members and takes seriously baptism's covenant; on the con-
trary, confirmation can be a stunning moment in anyone's life of faith,

---

1. From the last line of Mary Oliver's poem "The Summer Day" in *New and Selected Poems* (Boston:
Beacon Press, 1992).

2. BCP 412.

particularly perhaps for those who were baptized as infants or very young children and who, therefore, had no way of comprehending the covenant to which they were joined at the word of parents and sponsors. My bias is that the prayer book says what it means, and that the rite is best celebrated by and with those who have decided to enter into a process of mature, thoughtful reflection, prayer, and conversation about the meaning of the Baptismal Covenant and its intersection with their lives.

Which is why the unnamed woman and I had such a colossal non-meeting of the minds. She saw it as a rite of passage, but one without much content or, for that matter, meaning; it was time, the child had to be done, end of discussion. In retrospect, of course, I regret that I did not engage my telephone companion in further conversation, ask her for instance what confirmation meant to her now, about her own preparation and about the meaning and the memory of her confirmation. I also wonder about her daughter and what she might have thought about all of this.

I titled this article intentionally. I'm inviting you, as I have invited others of various ages and stages of life, as I might have invited my telephone caller, into a contemplation[3] of our "one wild and precious life," because preparing for Confirmation—or for Reception or for Reaffirmation of Baptismal Vows—entails, I believe, doing precisely that. When I was a baby, I had that "one wild and precious life" laid out ahead of me in one long mystery; I had no idea on the day of my baptism where that mystery would lead or what its content would be. I knew eleven years' worth on the day I was confirmed in my large Roman Catholic parish, but I hadn't been asked to consider my life up to that time in the light of my baptism, nor had I been invited to look ahead to contemplate what my life might be in the light of my confirmation. The church of my childhood, at least in my local circumstance, viewed confirmation very much in keeping with my later telephone caller. Our preparation consisted in memorization and testing. No contemplation or conversation considered.

But for Episcopalians who worship within the parameters of the 1979 BCP, things are different. Several years ago, when I was facilitating a group preparing for the rite in one of our Episcopal congregations, one of the young men asked to have a private conversation. We'd been spending

---

3. Don't you love etymology? The word contemplation is derived from the Latin *cum* + *templum* = "with place for observation/sacred space" or we might say something like "thinking with the community of the People of God."

several weeks reviewing and then discussing the baptismal promises, talking about the meaning and import of one's word in public, and about the step of making a public commitment or deciding now was not the time to make a public commitment to live one's life in accord with those vows. He had come into the group with his customary bright gusto, bristling with questions, engaging in friendly debate, supporting his friends, and impressing me with his grasp of the material, but now he had an issue best pursued privately. He'd been thinking about it a lot, he told me, and trying to pray about it, but he didn't know what to do. He had become convinced that the vows made a lot of sense as a template for a moral way of life, so had decided that he would ask to be confirmed and to confirm the vows others had once made on his behalf. But then he thought some more and wondered what if, at twenty-three or thirty-five, he changed his mind. A vow is a serious thing, he told me seriously, and he didn't want to make one in good faith, only later to break it.

His conundrum was real: He was the son of a Christian mother, an Episcopalian by tradition, and a Jewish father. Although he and his younger brother had been brought up in the Church with the consent of their father (who accompanied the rest of the family to services for Christian "high holidays"), he wondered if, as he grew older, went to college, got out into the world, his views of life in general and religious life in particular might change. Might he decide that his father's tradition was more in keeping with his older self? And if that were to happen, if he were to convert to Judaism, he would be breaking the vows he would have made on the day of his Confirmation. In the conversation that ensued, I assured him that he was right to ask his questions, that I was impressed with the seriousness with which he was indeed contemplating his "own wild and precious life" in conjunction with the vows, his honoring both his parents' traditions while also honoring his own self-understanding, and his thoughtful consideration of the gravity of giving his word. But I was also able to offer his own words back to him. "In good faith" means what it says. One enters into these vows believing to the best of one's abilities that these promises make sense as a way to live one's life at the time one pronounces them. A month later, I stood by his side, his mother and father behind him, hands on his shoulders, in our cathedral, as he reaffirmed the vows made for him at his baptism.

But there's a bit more to this story. On that same day, because in part of that conversation and conversations I had had with other members of his group both in and outside our meeting room, I stepped up to be received officially into the Episcopal Church. I had been practicing the Episcopal "way" for several years, but was still canonically Roman Catholic. The testimonies of these juniors in high school, their questions, their struggles, their construction of creedal statements that made sense to them, their ability to translate the language of the church into their daily lives and run with it, and in a peculiar way, their criticism of the church as they experienced it from adults in their lives, "convicted me" as we used to say. How was it I had been living my own life and how did I intend to order it in the future? I was already in virtually every way an Episcopalian and as I had taught them, those vows made the most sense to me. Given all of that, I could not *not* stand up to be counted.

When I have the privilege—and I do not type that glibly—to work with groups preparing to stand up to affirm publicly what they believe, I want to do several things with them. I have already mentioned much of the primary content:

- a review of the Baptismal Covenant with particular attention to how those promises are expressed in the Monday–Saturday portions of our lives: at home, at work, at play, at school, among friends, with folks who don't appeal;
- some time in conversation about what it means to give one's word in public about anything;
- some discussion about this incarnation of the Christian faith and practice: why Episcopal and not Methodist or Presbyterian or Roman Catholic; i.e., why throw in one's lot with us as opposed to another expression?
- a fair amount of exchange on their experience of the church in their lives and the lives of their role models; and
- the question of whether this step is the right one at this time in their lives. One year there was a senior in high school who was working hard to get an athletic scholarship to college, her only avenue to paying for her higher education. She explained to me and to the class that that meant she would be unable to participate in our discussions and for this reason felt it unwise to make a commitment to the process, which also meant that she could not prepare to be confirmed at this time. To their credit, the whole group did their best to change the meeting times to serve her schedule; nothing worked, so her decision stood.

Beyond these key points, our process ranges differently given the peculiar make-up and needs of each group or individual, and it has shifted a bit over the years given changes in the church itself and in the communities where the process has taken place. I always want to ensure that the questions that are raised—any questions and the more the better—are always addressed, if not always answered. One year, for instance, it became clear that this particular group of senior high students had been studying evolution. It turned them on; they were excited about what they were learning. I was appalled to discover that they were afraid that the Episcopal Church condemned that set of theories about the birth of the universe and life forms. They were relieved and impressed to learn something about the ways in which Episcopalians have traditionally read and continue to read and study the Bible. Questions about where the Church is with respect to suicide and sexuality and issues concerning social justice also come into and belong to the mix, not only from the youth, but also from their elders who are also preparing to reaffirm their own older vows.[4] It was also important, I learned early in my experience with such groups, to create a covenant together that would state our aims, our responsibilities, our time commitments, and our participation in the group, and which all would sign, signaling our accountability to one another and to the process itself.

We also regularly pursue such questions as:

- Do we really believe what we proclaim every Sunday in the celebration of the Holy Eucharist, and what does that mean for us?
- What does prayer do in our lives? Is it for God, for our neighbors or enemies, or for us?
- Who was God for us in our earliest memory of God? Can we trace how that image has changed over the years—be they 14 years or 45—and what prompted the changes? (I once had a 15 year old tell us that her earliest image of God was Big Bird, a large, soft, nurturing creature who taught her things and always welcomed her no matter what she'd done.)
- What does it mean that the Bible says and we claim to believe that we're made in the image and likeness of God? How do we mirror our

---

4. On occasion, I have facilitated groups of mixed ages which include 16 year olds and 40-somethings and even some who would call themselves "seniors"—a very rewarding experience as they learn a number of things they have in common, as well as questions they never would have believed they share and what they have to teach each other, not only about the faith, but about their own lives.

Creator: in our love, in our compassion, in our doing justice, in our creativity, in our passion? Or what do we make of Jesus' promise that he's with us always, and most certainly when we're gathered in his name?

- What might Annie Dillard have meant when she wrote: "When we go to church, we should all be wearing crash helmets. Ushers should issue life preservers and signal flares; they should lash us to our pews"?[5]

- What does it mean that all of us are called to a life of ministry? What is baptismal ministry and how do we live it out, not so much in doing churchy sorts of things like proclaiming the Word of God on a Sunday, or joining altar guild, or being Eucharistic ministers, or teaching children, worthy as each of these is? What does it mean in high school or at the office or at home? One of the things that became a part of the process for all of the groups with which I worked, was a letter written to me at the conclusion of our time together, telling me their decision—to be confirmed or not—and the reasons for their decision, as well as a description of one way they intended to live out their baptismal promises in the next year. One year, one of the juniors, a talented artist, decided to volunteer at a local retirement home as an artist-in-residence with an eye to helping these folks in the last stages of their lives to depict with paint or pastel or marker or charcoal some of the most important moments in their lives.

- What is sin anyway, and repentance? Why do they claim a space in the baptismal vows as well as in most of our public acts of worship? What's with the plural language: "**We** confess . . . **we** have sinned by what **we** have done. . . ."And, by the way, what's grace got to do with it?

- And many, many more.

The point, as my title suggests, is to spend some time contemplating our one wild and precious life, especially as individuals, but also as individuals in the community gathered. Where and when have our lives seemed to have been most in tune with those vows, and where and when not and why? How do these vows make sense in the mystery of our lives that is still undiscovered territory? We matter. Our lives matter. Our lives in Christ matter. The process of preparation for Confirmation, or for the allied rites, is a ripe time, it seems to me, for rediscovering what that means.

---

5. Annie Dillard, *Teaching a Stone to Talk* (New York: Harper & Row, 1982), 40.

John Chrysostom, that golden-tongued ancestor of ours, is credited with having said to the newly baptized:

> You are not only free, but also holy. Not only holy, but also just. Not only just, but also sons and daughters. Not only sons and daughters, but also heirs. Not only heirs, but also brothers and sisters of Christ. Not only brothers and sisters of Christ, but also joint heirs with him. Not only joint heirs, but also members. Not only members, but also the Temple. Not only the Temple, but also instruments of the Spirit. Blessed be God who alone does wonderful things.[6]

I want all of those who approach the rite to know this and, to the best of their abilities, to incarnate it. Or, to paraphrase Elizabeth Barrett Browning:

> Earth's crammed with heaven
> And every common bush alive with God.
> Only [we] who see take off our shoes;
> The rest sit around and pluck blackberries.[7]

I want us all to take off our shoes, astonished at being on Holy Ground, all the days of our lives.

• • •

Victoria L. Garvey is one of those proverbial lifelong learners. She has been teaching since she was called to tutor other six year olds in the first grade. Although she began her professional career as a high school teacher of French and Religious Studies, she has taught at virtually all stages, with the most extensive forays at the graduate level. After having taught at Seabury-Western Theological Seminary for twelve years in her academic field (theology of the Hebrew Bible and allied disciplines), she is now the Associate for Lifelong Christian Formation in the Episcopal Diocese of Chicago, a position that involves the formal and informal education of all ages, liturgical planning, preaching, writing, and the general work of helping this particular corner of the Body of Christ to grow and prosper. Her favorite responsibility and privilege is helping others to converse with the tradition and find a home for themselves there.

---

6. Quoted from Robert Brooks, "Post-Baptismal Catechesis," in Michael Merriman, ed., *The Baptismal Ministry and the Catechumenate* (New York: The Church Hymnal Corporation, 1990), 140–146.

7. Elizabeth Barrett Browning, "Aurora Leigh," (London: J. Miller, 1864).

CHAPTER 9

Confirmation and Sacraments in Latino Ministries

Tom Callard and Anthony Guillén

"What do I have to do so that my daughter/son can make their Confirmation here?" is frequently the first question asked at Latino/ Hispanic congregations as parents come to inquire at the church. That is followed by many other questions, such as: "How much does it cost to have my son/daughter confirmed here?"; "How many classes do we have to attend?"; "Do the godparents have to be married in the church in order to be our daughter's/son's godparent?" And often the big question is saved for last, "Is this church catholic?" The same questions are asked about baptism and first communion.

These questions might seem a bit strange to the reader, but they are very familiar to those of us who work in Latino ministries. These questions come as a result of the experience that many Latinos, both those from other countries as well as in this country, have had when they have approached the church about a sacrament. In fact it is not uncommon, even today, to find signs at the door of the parish office describing the requirements for sacraments, as well as the fee and the day of the month or week when such sacraments are available. Since we do not post this information on a sign, it makes sense that a person seeking a sacrament then needs to raise the questions themselves.

It would be an understatement to say that sacraments are important to Latinos. Not only are they a part of the connection with tradition and the religious Catholicism of Latin America, they are also strongly connected to the culture. One could almost say that the sacraments are more sacred as far as the family is concerned than the way the family relates to the church. Sacraments, especially baptism and confirmation along with the rite of first communion, are as much about family and the extended family of godparents and sponsors as they are about church and faith. They are intrinsically tied together and play a huge role in Latino culture. They also make for great photo opportunities. Many Latino homes proudly display pictures of their children dressed in white celebrating their Baptism, First Communion, and Confirmation. Families go to great expense to celebrate the event with a huge party. It is not uncommon for a baptism to wait for years until the family has the funds required to host the party properly.

Clergy who work in Latino ministries in the Episcopal Church understand well the role of the sacraments in the lives of the communities they serve. And they know that people will often come to our churches not necessarily seeking a church community or a place to find God, and not necessarily looking to deepen their relationship with Christ or improve their knowledge of the faith and the Bible and the traditions. Often they come because they are only looking for sacraments.

It is important, therefore, for clergy in Latino congregations, and those in Anglo congregations serving in communities where many Latinos live, to be conscious of how they respond to the people coming to the door to ask: "What do I have to do so my daughter/son can make their Confirmation here?" We do not want to make the Episcopal church the catholic (small "c") church people go to because it is easier to get their children confirmed or baptized than the other Catholic church. And we do not want to fall into a kind of simony, which is defined by the Catechism of the Catholic Church as "the buying or selling of spiritual things" and refers to buying or selling of the sacraments.

Church-savvy Latinos will come to the church often expecting to arrange for sacramental services to be performed at the date and time of their choosing when it best accommodates their family's needs, at the cheapest price,[1] and with the least commitment of time. These are parents who know that they have a moral and religious obligation to make sure that their children receive the three essential sacraments: Baptism, Confirmation, and First Communion. And the elder women in the family are constantly reminding them that they are not good parents unless their children have completed all three. And so the parents, often the mother, taking their responsibility serious, will go from one congregation to another, seeking a congregation that will assist them in providing the

---

1. Many Roman Catholic churches charge a fee for the administration of sacraments such as baptism, confirmation, and funerals.

three sacraments they have been raised to believe are the essentials of the faith and the requirements of the Church.

To the Roman Catholic Church's credit, most parishes have strict rules that a family has to meet in order to have their child baptized, their young person confirmed, or make their first communion. The primary obligation is several years of catechetical study, which for many parents seems like an unnecessary burden. On top of this, a fee is often charged for the program. Due to the two- or three-year-long program, many Latinos seek other options. That is where the Episcopal Church comes in. Word spreads quickly from family to family and *comadre* to *comadre* that the Episcopal Church does not require such long study, and often does it for free.

While this is certainly not true of every Latino who comes to our church, it happens enough in some communities that we should be prepared for when people come to inquire about the sacraments. And we should understand how to work with the families without turning them away, use the opportunity to invite them in, and if possible, involve them in our tradition. After all, they want tradition.

It would be so much easier just to accommodate people by giving them what they want, and there are some congregations in Latino ministries in the Episcopal Church that are happy to dispense the sacraments and ask for little or no commitment in return. We used to call them sacramental mills. And unfortunately, clergy, lay leaders, and bishops who are involved will often do little to stop the practice or help to encourage the families to think of their faith beyond the mentality of just getting the three key sacraments over for their children's spiritual development.

Like all congregations, those in Latino ministries in the Episcopal Church want to grow and bring in more people. It is a reality that many congregations in Latino ministries work under an implicit or explicit deadline from their diocese, which says that they must be self-sufficient in three to five years or they will be closed. There is tremendous pressure to have a lot of people at Mass. So when the opportunity presents itself to have your church full of people on Sunday (and especially for the bishop's visitation), churches take shortcuts that circumvent the hard work that goes into building a parish and developing lifelong disciples in the faith.

We are reminded of a story of a Latino congregation that had so many confirmations one year that assistants volunteered to hold up the bishop's arms in order to finish the laying on of hands. That congregation had thousands of members on its books due to the large number of baptisms and confirmations they held. Saturdays were bustling with one service after another, since many Latinos prefer to have their child baptized on Saturday so they can have a party afterwards. And because of the fees charged for each baptism, first communion, or confirmation, the congregation had a steady income. Their ministry gave families the opportunity to get their children dressed in white to take celebratory pictures. And all of this came through a robust ministry of offering sacraments.

Confirmation was especially fruitful for the parish because confirmation means that the bishop will be present and that brings more people to church. The church would be very full for every confirmation service, the bishop would be happy to see that the church was full, and from all appearances the Latino ministry was growing. But then on the following Sunday after the confirmation service, when the church went back to its regular attendance, most of those who had been confirmed did not come back. Their families would disappear because they now had in their hand the "required" confirmation certificates and the photos of the sacrament and the "required" party. So it would not be until the next child was ready to celebrate their confirmation or first communion, or the baby was ready to be baptized that they would appear again.

The true membership of this church was, in fact, very small. Few parishioners pledged, and only a small group of leaders participated in any regular study and training. It seemed fairly clear that there was no process to incorporate new families into the life of the congregation, nor were the families really encouraged to stay. On the one hand the church looked like it was thriving, vibrant, and active because of all the confirmations, but the reality was that the thriving ministry of confirmations did not translate into a church that was healthy or sustainable or growing.

Latino congregations need to be honest with themselves about wanting to grow their membership at all costs, and examine what role sacraments play in their strategy to grow the congregation. We suggest that a common set of guidelines should be developed across the Latino ministries on the Episcopal Church and define our expectations for those who come to participate in our sacramental ministries.

While it may not be possible to have a one-size-fits-all agreement that is adapted by every Latino congregation, we can do much more to distinguish ourselves from just being the other "small c" catholics, where it is easy to get their children their sacraments.

Our guidelines have to be stringent. We need to expect a commitment before and after the confirmation happens. We need to expect those preparing for Confirmation to attend classes, study what they are presented, and to be tested on what they have learned. And we expect students and families to participate in the activities and ministries of the church in addition to coming to Mass on Sunday. And of course we expect them to be at the Mass, and we need to somehow take their attendance weekly to see that they are there.

We frequently ask so little of the families because we do not want to scare them into running away or returning to their old church.

We also seldom provide a quality, well-thought-out confirmation class, often citing that it is due to lack of printed resources in Spanish. But if we were honest with ourselves, we would find that many of our youth confirmands are actually English speakers. We do not give meaningful roles or ministries to those who are confirmed which might involve them in the life of the church. In the case of Spanish-dominant youth, it is true that there are few resources available; it is our hope that some quality bilingual resources can be made available for this ever-growing ministry.

We must also work to convince families that there is more to faith than just the moment of the sacrament, and that the sacraments are part of an ongoing process of formation, discipleship, and salvation in a person's life, but not the whole piece. Of course it is not only Latino families who send their children to be confirmed without upholding a larger connection to the faith or the church. Everywhere confirmation classes are full of young people who are simply there to fulfill an obligation, and they will disappear as soon as the classes are finished.

Perhaps we need to de-emphasize the sacraments and instead focus on other ways to also celebrate the spirituality found in our understanding of the sacraments. For example, Confirmation is making a mature commitment to Christ. The mature commitment is at the heart of our understanding of the sacrament. What kind of a commitment is a teenager able to understand? Perhaps a huge commitment to Jesus or to the vows of their baptism is a little bit too much for most teenagers. So how could we augment the mature commitment of confirmation with a series of additional, smaller commitments that are made as one is growing and maturing in their life?

For those looking to celebrate their faith publicly, what if we had a rite that celebrated every time a person made a new commitment to something? You would come to church and with the witness of your community, with your sponsors at your side and in the presence of almighty God, you would commit yourself to a new grade in school, a new job, a new drivers' license, a new relationship, a new ministry in the church, or even a new diet, any of those things that you want to be blessed and confirmed. You could make commitments throughout the course of life, starting at adolescence when most people today are confirmed. And with every commitment, you would proclaim your faith in Jesus Christ and reaffirm your renunciation of evil.

We could explain to families seeking the sacrament of confirmation that in addition to confirmation—or as an alternative to confirming your teenage son or daughter—we offer a whole series of smaller confirmation possibilities for every mature commitment a person is prepared to make. Sundays at church would be active and alive with Christians coming forward for blessings, and in the process we could be connecting what happens in church on Sunday with what goes on for people the rest of their lives.

In the context of Latino ministry, to de-emphasize the sacrament of confirmation would help people think beyond the three-sacrament model of spiritual completeness and realize that there can be many wonderful ways to receive God's blessing while committing themselves to their faith. Instead of just the photos and the memories of that day when their child stood with the bishop to be confirmed, they would have a lifetime of memories of confirmations and celebrations at different places and moments in life.

One last thing to consider is how the practice of reception could also help create possibilities for congregants to think beyond sacraments and engage in a well-structured spiritual program. Reception is fairly new in the church, having appeared for the first time in the 1979 BCP. Perhaps because reception is not a sacrament, there is less excitement about it on the part of Latinos. In our experience, people seldom come to the church for the first time looking to be received. There are not the same well-produced programs for reception as there are for confirmation. It is not easy to build up excitement in the community about reception, the way you can in a Latino community about the sacramental ministries. Yet, there seems to be a correlation between adult reception and having more educated and committed members. And reception is a well-developed practice in many parts of the Anglican Communion.

Currently, Reception and Confirmation generally happen at the same service, but the liturgy is almost entirely focused on Confirmation. We would suggest that a separate service be created similar to the one in the BCP of the Church of the Province of Southern Africa called "The Admission of Baptized Communicants from Other Churches into Communicant Membership of the Church of the Province of Southern Africa." The service calls upon those to be admitted to declare their faith; acknowledge the catholicity of the church; accept the three-fold ministry and sacraments; accept the discipline and teaching of the church; and commit to its worship, work, and witness.

The BCP 1979 gives us very little direction in regard to Reception, except to say that "adults . . . are also expected to make a public affirmation of their faith and commitment to the responsibilities of their Baptism in the presence of a bishop and to receive the laying on of hands." What is clear is that the words that the bishop says state two things clearly: "we recognize you" and "we receive you." So common practice is that clergy utilize reception as the alternative to confirmation for adults who have already been confirmed. These adults are persons who have often come back to the church and want to make that public affirmation of faith or to state publicly that they want to join the Episcopal Church.

Part of the strength of reception is that it happens in the context of the bishop's visit, just like confirmation. But unlike what we often see in youth confirmation, reception almost always involves adults who have fully committed themselves to their church and their faith. What a wonderful way to celebrate and recognize adult spirituality in Latino congregations, where almost one hundred percent of Latino congregants are new to the Episcopal Church, to prepare people and present them and thank God for their presence with us.

The preparation for Reception, just as with Confirmation, ought to be guided by a clear set of expectations regarding how to best prepare people, what to teach them, and how to evaluate their progress in learning and formation as Episcopalians. In addition to teaching people, reception could also be an amazing opportunity to learn from those who are being received. This is especially true in a Latino ministry context, where people are coming into our church from a variety of different contexts all of which are different. We could have part of the reception process be hearing about people's stories and their journey of faith that brought them to the church.

As the Episcopal Church continues to grow and expand its ministry with Latinos, we welcome the opportunity of having many more people knock on our doors in the future, coming to inquire about who we are and what we have to offer. It is an amazing thing anytime someone comes to the door of the church, regardless of what brings them there, and we must never neglect to show hospitality to them, for in that way we will entertain angels. Perhaps starting with the Latino cultural understanding about the sacraments, we must do all we can to help them bear fruit in their lives, become involved in the community, and find God through the rich tradition and culture of our church, including the sacraments but also beyond them and in addition to them.

• • •

The Reverend Canon Tom Callard is the Canon at Christ Church Cathedral in Springfield, Massachusetts, also serving as the Missioner for Hispanic Ministries in the Diocese of Western Massachusetts. For several years a missionary in Honduras, he has since served in several congregations that are English and Spanish speaking. He helped start the Instituto de Liderazgo, a training program for Lay Spanish Speakers in the Diocese of Los Angeles. Married to a woman originally from Honduras, they have three children.

• • •

The Reverend Canon Anthony Guillén has been the Missioner for Latino/Hispanic Ministries at the Episcopal Church Center since 2005. As Missioner, he developed the Episcopal Church's Strategic Vision for Reaching Latinos/Hispanics, which was adopted at General Convention in 2009. Guillén previously served for thirteen years as rector of All Saints Church in Oxnard, California, where he led the congregation to become a vibrant bilingual/bicultural parish in the Diocese of Los Angeles. In his early years in ministry, Guillén was a youth minister, a missionary in the Diocese of Western Mexico where he established two missions and worked as diocesan youth coordinator. He was named Honorary Canon of the Catedral de San Juan el Evangelista in San Juan, Puerto Rico and Catedral del Señor in Quito, Ecuador.

CHAPTER 10

Christian Identity

Prince G. Singh

I was confirmed on July 7, 1977 at St. Andrew's Kirk, a Church of South India congregation in what was Madras then and now is Chennai in India. There were twenty-five of us confirmands, as I recall. I was fifteen. When the Bishop laid hands on my head and prayed me into that amazing prayer of confirmation, I was visibly moved. "My life matters to God," was the clarity I had as a confirmed person. My life had always mattered to God, of course, and Confirmation was my appropriation of that truth. The baptismal reminder that we are all made good and in the image of God took me to a place of responsibility as a follower of Christ. Such a place of responsibility moved me to a self-understanding that was about becoming a follower of Christ and hence a leader in the community.

Christian leadership is about building beloved community where the formation of self and engagement of the other commingle in a reflective praxis of the Church's mission—to restore all people to unity with God and each other in Christ. Christian leadership then is a constant quest to rebalance the restoration of unity with God and God's reign while also making sure unity is at the relational level with one another. Therefore, the call for Christian leadership is about clarifying one's identity as a child of God and one's vulnerability in seeking reconciliation with other people, creation, and all manner of life. Building beloved community is a core drive of Christian leadership because it seeks the very heart and face of God. It is reflected not in uniformity but unity, not in homogeneity but in diversity, and not in solace but in empowerment. This is my prayer:

One step at a time in these moments of opportunity and challenge
Fifty years after a dreamer dreamed new possibility into new reality.
Remind us to do our part to build beloved community.

Help us, Beloved, Holy Other,

To be still and know that you are here

Help us to embrace your love and our responsibility

Help us to embrace you in the strange other

Help us do our part to heal this body of Christ and a hurting world

Help us to forgive, repent and receive forgiveness

May every encounter be holy!

With every decision we consider and make

Every choice we make to reduce our harmful footprint

Divestment we make to reduce future harm to our island home

Help us do our part to heal this hurting earth

Help us do our part to heal ourselves, our souls

Heal us of every sense of loss and grief

Loss of loved ones,

Loss of the familiar,

And the grief caused by failed expectations

Heal us of every encumbrance that keeps our reality powerful
      and your possibility weak . . .

Holy Other, Beloved One,

Ages after you stretched the skies as you stretched your hands
      on hardwood and dreamed a beloved possibility

Help us do our part to take one moment at a time

To move with faith, hope and love

To build, build, and build,

A beloved community here and now. Amen.

Confirmation to me is the Church's creative impulse to reflect her deepest yearning to proclaim resurrection in all forms of abundant life within a formative framework that would be intentionally replicated from generation to generation. While Confirmation is assumed for its power as a ritual of initiation, that aspect of initiation is more theologically characterized in baptismal theology. Baptism is really the ritual initiation into God's beloved community where all are reminded as Jesus was about their inherent beloved quality in the eyes of God. This fundamental sacrament is clearly the cornerstone of Christian identity. It is out of such a Christian identity of being God's beloved that all aspects of disciple-ship including Christian piety, worship, ethics, character, and leadership development emanate.

My college years at Madras Christian College were formative years. I got involved in leadership in the Student Christian Movement and we were engaged in the study of scripture, prayer, and social action. We also had a lot of fun engaging the world as we saw it, especially through music and skits. My encounter with the vulnerable of the world was shaped in the context of a leprosy clinic in the outskirts of Tambaram, where my college was. It was here that I saw the face of Christ in the face of broken vulnerable persons with the variety of disfigurements that accompanied this disease. It was during those days that I learned to differentiate between the disease and the person. I came to realize that these were children of God, not lepers, since leprosy was the disease and not the person. I learned to address them as persons with leprosy or as leprosy patients. When they touched me I realized Christ himself was touching me. Later, when I was in discernment for the priesthood, I would spend an entire year serving as a chaplain, visiting them every Sunday evening in a leprosy colony located in outskirts of the city of Madras.

The Church must constantly seek spiritual leaders passionately. It is fundamental that Christian leaders are first followers of Jesus the Christ with a dynamic walk with him. Everything, including qualifications and skills, is secondary to this fundamental assumption. A question that I ask at every Confirmation liturgy in the diocese is: "Do you renew your commitment to Jesus Christ?" The response: "I do, and with God's grace I will follow him as my Savior and Lord." Every disciple of Christ who seeks to be a leader in the Church and the world would benefit from paying attention to this. The Church is best when everyone works with one common purpose: to restore all people to unity with God and each other in Christ. That is our ultimate mission. To this end, the formation of Christian leaders is crucial to accomplishing this mission. I see Confirmation as a primary portal in the formation and development of Christian leaders for Church and society.

Lay people, including my mother, a bunch of friends in college, and eventually clergy, fundamentally influenced my journey with Jesus Christ. I see this as a common pattern of being drawn to be followers of Christ where the primary conduits of the grace of Jesus are Christian leaders who have a dynamic spiritual life. Lay people who take their baptismal vows seriously, which they appropriate and confirm at confirmation, are a significant "entre" to the Christian's fundamental task of sharing the good news of Christ. This is also the first of the Five Marks of Mission that the worldwide Anglican Communion has embraced—to proclaim the Good News of the Kingdom.

The Church must also seek leaders who are formed to be thoughtful in their engagement with their context. One of the important aspects of leadership is discernment of the best path forward with as much information as possible. Organizational structure works best when it functions through a missional lens that assumes that all the baptized are participating in healthy ways. The Episcopal Church is a healthy blend of democratic processes within a hierarchical structure to make things work. While all opinions are welcomed, every opinion cannot be discerned as consequential to decision making particularly. That would be democracy gone awry or, as Aristotle would call it, mob rule.

Anthony De Mello tells the story of a grandpa and his grandson taking their donkey to the market to sell. Grandpa was riding the donkey and as they went through the first village, they heard people murmuring about how it was such a terrible thing that the old man was making the youngster walk while he rode comfortably. As they left the village, grandpa got off the donkey and put the little fellow on it. They passed the second village and they heard murmuring again. This time they heard people complaining how terrible it was that the little fellow had no respect for elders and was letting the old man walk while he rode comfortably. As they left the village the grandson got off the donkey. The story continues with them going through a third village. This time both were quite tired and were riding on the donkey and people started complaining that they are such heartless people making the creature a real beast of burden. Finally grandpa and grandson decided to carry the donkey to the market! Formation of leadership is mostly about making good choices, not necessarily popular ones. The moral framework to inform these choices has to be formed early on in the lives of young people. This is primarily why confirmation is an important formation experience to prepare young people as well as adults to take their place as leaders in the world, which God loved enough to send us a savior.

. . .

The Right Reverend Prince G. Singh was born in Chenaii, Tamil Nadu India. He graduated from Madras Christian College, Tambaram, and Union Biblical Seminary, both in India. He was ordained a priest in the Church of South India (Anglican Communion) in 1990 and served congregations in rural South India. Bishop Singh has served as the VIII bishop in the Episcopal Diocese of Rochester, New York since his election in 2008. As bishop, he walks with the 47 diverse parishes that comprise the diocese.

PART III

DULY PREPARED

For by grace you have been saved through faith, and this is not your own doing; it is the gift of God—not the result of works, so that no one may boast. For we are what he has made us, created in Christ Jesus for good works, which God prepared beforehand to be our way of life.

—Ephesians 2:8–10

CHAPTER 11

Everything You Need to Know to Be Confirmed

Laura Darling

I n my role representing *Confirm not Conform*, I've had the opportunity to talk to many people about how they prepare people for confirmation. There's one conversation in particular that I return to again and again when I consider how we may be approaching confirmation in a way that completely defeats its purpose.

I was at General Convention and talking with a priest I'd known a long time, now a rector in my former diocese. He wasn't interested in *CnC*, saying he already had a program and system he liked, so I asked him about it. He explained how many weeks it took and the topics he normally covered. But then he said, "I can teach someone everything they need to know to be confirmed in a day if I have to. I just sit them down and talk for a few hours."

"Ah," I said.

And I thought, there in a nutshell are some of the essential problems with the way we approach confirmation today.

It's not the "I can sit them down and talk for a few hours" part that's most disturbing to me, although that is problematic. It's the part where we believe that we can "teach someone everything they need to know to be confirmed." Because I have come to learn that confirmation has little to do with having the right information.

As the prayer book says, those baptized at an early age are to be confirmed "when they are ready and have been duly prepared." But what does being duly prepared look like? How do we duly prepare someone for confirmation? That is the sticking point.

We need to start by asking what we think we are preparing people *for*. One of the problems with confirmation as we currently practice it is that we confuse confirmation with other tasks: with becoming an (young) adult, becoming an Episcopalian, or joining a church. It's clear from our Prayer Book that confirmation is none of those things. Instead, those being confirmed are expected:

- to make a mature public affirmation of their faith;
- to make a commitment to the responsibilities of their baptism;
- to receive the laying on of hands by the bishop.

Of these, I would argue that the first step is the most germane to our preparations. It is in the ability to make a mature public affirmation of one's faith that one is then able to make a genuine commitment to the responsibilities of one's baptism.

Here is the crucial point: you cannot sit a person down and "teach them what they need to know" to make a mature affirmation of faith—whether it be in a day, or weeks, or any length of time—because a mature affirmation of faith cannot be taught. It needs to come from within the person being confirmed. The thing that people most need to know about when they are confirmed is what they believe and why they believe it. And in exploring that, we can help them see how and where that fits in the Christian tradition.

If we understand confirmation in this way, then it is clear why my colleague's comment on confirmation preparation was so disturbing to me. You cannot "teach someone what they need to know" to be a mature Christian. To make that statement shows a profound misunderstanding about the nature of confirmation and about the kind of support we need to provide.

As I have thought more deeply about the nature of confirmation over these past five years, I've come to see issues that surround confirmation and suffuse our conversations about it, making it difficult for us to focus on confirmation's essential task and nature, and almost impossible for us to assume our proper role in helping confirmands be duly prepared.

Let's start by examining the assumption that the entirety of confirmation preparation takes place during confirmation classes.

The reality of bishops' schedules and regional confirmations has the unfortunate effect of requiring confirmands to be able to affirm their faith on a deadline. And so we set up our classes a certain number of weeks ahead of the bishop's visit with a certain number of sessions covering a certain number of topics, and call this "confirmation preparation."

But that is an erroneous description. It was only recently that I realized "confirmation preparation" is the entirety of a person's life and faith development until they are confirmed. I'm embarrassed to realize how many years I thought confirmands would be dependent upon *me* as their confirmation class leader to provide them with what they needed so they could undertake this step. What we call "confirmation preparation" is more properly a time set aside for confirmands to explore the preparation that has been taking place all along: in their experience of worship, in their studies, in their families, and in their communities of faith.

We need to expand our understanding of confirmation preparation to include not only all the spiritual formation we offer (and not just in the run-up to confirmation), but also the ways in which one's faith is developed through family and friends, culture, community, and personal experience. How can we help people prepare throughout their lives so it doesn't simply offer a mature-affirmation-of-faith cram session before the bishop's visitation? Or more accurately, how can we help unpack those faith experiences that people have been having all along so when the time comes, confirmands are able to see how their lives have been suffused by God's love, Christ's presence, and the Spirit's leading, and can articulate that experience?

Another issue that I see with youth confirmation programs in particular is that we want to stuff in as much information, spiritual preparation, social justice, and general goodness with an overlay of denominational cheerleading as we can. My hunch is that we do that because we figure this is our one shot. But I am concerned that if we try to make confirmation do everything, all we're going to succeed in doing is making people think Christian formation is being force-fed every dish on the Thanksgiving buffet. Even if the dishes are delicious, people are still going to be sick of eating them. And chances are they're not going to want to eat any of it again for a long time.

The fact is there is far more to share than we can possible digest in a brief series of confirmation classes. Christian history, spiritual practices, theology, Scripture: there's so much good stuff it's hard to know even where to begin. But just because there is an abundance doesn't mean everyone is required to eat everything all at once. We wouldn't invite someone to Thanksgiving dinner and say, "Eat this whole turkey! Now the green beans! Don't forget the mince pie! Oh, there's pumpkin, too!" Doing so is hostile, not hospitable.

Our job isn't to force-feed; our job is to invite, to set the table, to offer the food. We can bring out the old family recipes or try new ones. We can recommend a dish to sample and ask what people think. We can ask people to bring their own favorite family dishes. But we're not going to get everything in. Let's stop trying. Save the leftovers and send them home with the guests. Maybe they'll eat them. Maybe they'll stay in the back of the refrigerator. That's not up to us.

I suspect, however, that people are more likely to return for another dinner if they don't worry that they're going to be sick afterwards. We need to be hospitable and make confirmation classes as delicious as possible. I suspect if we do so, people will come for—and with—Thanksgiving year after year.

But what do we need to teach? As I'm sure we are all aware, there are things we as clergy think are deeply important that are in fact irrelevant to the objective of helping people make a mature affirmation of faith. I've taught many a class on the Anglican Reformation, which of course I find fascinating, but who am I kidding? You don't actually need to know the first thing about the Elizabethan Settlement to be a faithful Christian. I suspect a lot of us fill our confirmation classes with information that we happen to find interesting, or perhaps because it allows us to display our expertise, but with little thought as to whether it is relevant to people's lives or questions.

It's not that imparting information in an effective way is either trivial or easy. But the information we share about our faith and tradition needs to be in conversation with the lived faith experience of those who are exploring whether or not to be confirmed. The importance of the information is in illuminating or deepening the articulation of confirmands' faith, a faith that has been developing throughout their lives. Our expertise can still be brought to bear, but it may require us to be more nimble on our feet as we seek to connect the lived experience of confirmands with our knowledge of Scripture, history, theology, and tradition, recognizing that the responsibility for confirmation preparation does not rest entirely upon our shoulders. Can we let go of that burden and trust that the Holy Spirit leads people to a mature faith even if they know nothing about the Chicago-Lambeth Quadrilateral, as wonderful as it is?

Here's the next assumption I'd like to examine: Why do we assume that someone who wants to be confirmed needs additional preparation? What if we discover after sitting down with someone that she is perfectly able to make a mature affirmation of faith today? Do we still say, "Great! Here's the schedule of our confirmation program! You are required to attend if you want to be confirmed"? Or do we say, "Great! It's clear you are ready to be confirmed. Confirmation is on this date"?

As a curriculum developer, this question is a challenge to me. After all, everyone can learn something. But if we truly believe that the expectation is for someone to be able to make a mature affirmation of her faith, and the person in front of us already can, then what are we having classes for?

In a complete departure from my objections to the notion that "I can teach a person everything they need to know in a day," I firmly believe there are plenty of people in our churches who can beautifully articulate their faith with no help from us whatsoever. There are people who have been "duly prepared" without any classes from us. Perhaps the best thing we can do in that situation is to humbly listen and then ask what we can do to support them.

At the same time, even for those with a mature faith, our spiritual formation and growth needs to be ongoing. But we need to be clear about what we are having classes for. I would argue that any confirmation program we offer needs to have the object of confirmation in mind: that we are assisting confirmands to make a mature public affirmation of their faith. For those who are already able to do that, we need to be mindful both of what we can offer to help them continue and deepen their exploration, and be humble in knowing they are already prepared and in receiving what they have to offer.

I would like to offer five considerations on how we can approach confirmation preparation in a way that allows confirmands at all levels of faith development to do the work of affirming their faith.

1. **Create a safe and healthy environment for exploration.** Have the group set its own ground rules. Stay mindful of group dynamics. Allow laughter. Always leave room for doubt and questions. Listen.

2. **Find ways to connect information *about* faith with exploration of *lived* faith.** For example, it is a great thing to explain to people about different forms of prayer, but a far more practical application is we allow people to try out those forms of prayer—and then discuss which forms they liked and didn't like, and why. And when in doubt, bear in mind that information is probably less important than you think.

3. **Answers are less helpful than sitting with the questions.** When we provide answers, we keep people in a state of immaturity. Wrestling with one's faith *is* an act of faith. As we assist people in articulating their faith, it may be that our role is to keep putting forward the questions and not working towards a speedy resolution of doubt or uncertainty. Remember that the opposite of faith is not doubt, but certainty. It may be that in providing answers we are in fact killing people's faith.

4. **Be mindful of the broad spectrum of faith in the Christian tradition.** We ask people to affirm *their* faith, not ours. Along with not providing quick answers, I also think it is important not to limit faith to our own preference. Are we aware of the breadth of Christianity? Can we point to Scriptures or theologians that illuminate the path someone is on, even if it is not our own?

5. **Not getting confirmed is also a faithful choice.** One of the original reasons the creators of *Confirm not Conform* developed the program was that they felt it was vital for confirmation to be a genuine choice, and that those who chose not to be confirmed should also be honored for the work and discernment they had done. We need to take confirmation seriously enough to take no for an answer, and to honor and respect those who make that choice. Despite the bishop's scheduled visit, faith does not work to a deadline.

In confirmation, we need to respect, honor, and recognize the faith of those being confirmed. The essential element of confirmation is that people are given the opportunity to make that choice to stand in front of the community and say, "Yes. I claim this faith for myself. I may not know everything about it, but I choose to follow the Way of Christ, and I do so of my own free will."

One of the concerns I have about the canons that require confirmation for vestry members is that it may have the unintended consequence of making it *less* likely that confirmation is a mature affirmation of faith, *less* likely to be an honest choice, and not more. "We need to get you confirmed," I can imagine us saying—and have heard people say—without consideration for the fact that confirmation is to the church's good *not* because those confirmed can now do stuff for us, but because it is to the church's benefit to have mature Christians.

Do we want mature Christians to be on our vestries? Of course. But then I hear, "I can teach someone everything they need to be confirmed in a day." I hear a bishop tell a group of confirmands that "many of you are getting confirmed because your parents want you too—and that's OK." I hear of adults in our parishes who went through *pro forma* confirmation classes without once reflecting on their faith. And I worry that we don't prepare people to confirm their faith. We prepare people to have confirmation done to them.

If I did not know this, I might feel differently. But it is terribly easy to slip into getting people "done." It still happens all the time. And so, as an avowed supporter of confirmation who takes the rite and the sacrament very seriously, I am exceedingly wary of connecting confirmation to our leadership needs.

We need to bear in mind that our goal for church leaders is faithfulness and maturity, not *pro forma* confirmation. In an ideal world, those two things go together. In our current practice, I can only see that making confirmation the bar we ask people to clear will only serve to lower it.

• • •

The Reverend Laura Darling is the Senior Director for Home and Community Based Services with Episcopal Senior Communities in the San Francisco Bay area and has been the Managing Director of *Confirm not Conform* since 2008. Ordained in 2001, she previously served as the Episcopal Chaplain at Kenyon College and as the Associate Rector and youth minister at Christ Church, Alameda, California, as well as working as a Kiva Fellow with microfinance institutions in Uganda.

CHAPTER 12

Practical Matters

Jenifer Lee Gamber

This is to certify that on June 3, 1979 we did receive
Jenifer C. Lee into the communion and fellowship of this
branch of Christ's Holy Catholic Church; The said person
having already received the apostolic rite of confirmation.

—*Signed by The Reverend John L. Kater, Jr. and
The Right Reverend Paul Moore*

So reads my certificate of confirmation in the Diocese of New York. It is the Episcopal Church's *official* response to my choice before God, the people of Christ Episcopal Church, and the bishop of New York to reaffirm my love for God, God's son, and the Holy Spirit. I was thirteen. I'd add that, unlike so many youth then and today, I was not taking on a faith that my parents had chosen for me when I was an infant. My parents had indeed taken seriously their responsibility for seeing that I was brought up in the Christian faith and life *and* believed that it was my choice to baptized. I was baptized when I was eight years old.

I remember choosing to be baptized. In practical terms it was to receive communion—to partake fully in the Holy mysteries of the Church. I was part of the church family and wanted to be at the Table, too. My parents and church modeled what it meant to be a Christian. I went to nearly every church event. I served people outside the church alongside my friends and adults. I said the Nicene Creed every Sunday. I knew what it meant to continue in the apostles' teaching and fellowship, to repent and return to the Lord when I sinned, to proclaim the Good News, to love my neighbor as myself, and strive for justice. I wanted to make a commitment to God, to become a member of the household of God, and to be sealed as Christ's own forever. It was fitting that I was baptized on All Saints Day, a feast day I treasure.

My baptism and confirmation is the foundation of my theology of baptism, my approach to confirmation, and belief in the ministry of all the baptized. So, here's my story.

On Sunday morning, November 1, 1974, the procession into the church began—the cross, the torchbearers, and then my brother and me and our friends, followed by the choir and the priest. As we processed by the baptismal font, each child poured a Dixie™ cup of water into the baptismal waters. When it was time for the baptism, we all processed back to the font. I was baptized and on that day I received Eucharist for the first time! I truly belonged.

I celebrated the Eucharist with my faith community, being fed alongside those who'd shown me God's love through teaching, sharing their faith and working together in the ministries of the Church inside and outside of the church walls. Did I fully understand what I was taking on when saying the Apostle's Creed? Agreeing to be sealed as Christ's own forever? Committing to a life in Christ? I understood as much as any of us are able. Did I have unanswered questions? Yes, and I still do. Even so, I wanted forever to be a member of the body of Christ and to follow Jesus.

In the following years in my family and faith community, I continued to witness God's love, learn our sacred stories, and participate in the ministry of the Church. I developed relationships with adults; we called one another friends. As was the custom at our church, when I turned thirteen, five years later, it was time to take on an intentional and concentrated study of our faith with others to prepare to reaffirm my baptismal promises. Our rector, John Kater, was in the middle of writing a book, *A Faith for Teenagers*, which we used as our text. It was about mystery, prayer, bread, Christian life, falling short of our promises through honest conversation, and more. With a shared book we explored, questioned, and doubted together. The people of Christ Church knew that we had a relationship with God and our own authentic experiences in the world. We were theologians and were encouraged to ask the big questions.

The day came to be confirmed. I don't remember making an active choice to be confirmed. It was a natural progression of my life of faith, a part of the journey presented by the Church. I believed in God's love; I knew the Church as a loving family that cared about people beyond its doors; I wanted to continue the journey. What I remember about the confirmation liturgy is the sermon—my brother was the lost sheep, and Bishop Moore used his wooden crozier to bring him back to the fold. I remember kneeling, feeling the bishop's heavy hands on my shoulders, and receiving his blessing.

I *re*-affirmed my faith in front of a community that showed me God's love. I felt I'd grown up a bit more, rooting myself more deeply, and the people of Christ Church recognized I was becoming an adult. From the bishop's presence, I learned I was part of a community beyond Christ Church. I didn't stop going to church or learning about God after I was confirmed. God and the Church were an integral part of who I was. Above all else, it was where I was loved.

I tell this story because my affirming the Baptismal Covenant informs my ministry as a layperson.[1] It informs the place I believe baptism and confirmation has in Christian life and the Church and is foundational to what I believe to be important in the catechetical process of preparing for confirmation.

DESIGNING A CONFIRMATION PREPARATION PROCESS

Confirmation, as written in the *Constitution and Canons of the Episcopal Church*, is a "mature public affirmation of [their] faith and commitment to the responsibilities of [their] Baptism." It is a public proclamation of a personal relationship with God as expressed in the Baptismal Covenant. The confirmand is saying, "I give my heart to God" and "I promise to live as a disciple of Christ." Preparing a candidate to proclaim this relationship requires opportunities to understand that living relationship (to whom are we giving our heart?) and intentional commitment (what does it mean to follow Christ in our lives?), and to discern whether the candidates want to affirm that faith. Confirming one's faith means committing to a transforming and radical life in Christ.

A number of essays in this book address the theological issues of confirmation and its place in the life of the Episcopal Church. While this essay puts these issues largely aside, the proposed guidelines for building a process for preparing candidates for confirmation reflects the following

---

1. Close readers might realize that I was baptized five years before the 1979 Book of Common Prayer was adopted. At my baptism, Christ Church was using a provisional Book of Common Prayer known as the "Zebra" Book with the same baptismal liturgy that is used today.

liturgically normative understandings of baptism as reflected in the liturgy
of Holy Baptism in the Book of Common Prayer:

> Baptism is full initiation into the body of Christ.
>
> Baptism is indissoluble.

Confirmation, then, is not receiving a person as a *full* member of the
Church. Every baptized person partakes fully in the Baptismal Covenant
and is given the gifts necessary for Christian ministry. Thus, choosing not
to be confirmed does not "undo" baptism. We are marked as Christ's own
forever. With this understanding, and in light of the normative practice of
baptizing infants, confirmation is an act in which a person *owns the Baptismal Covenant for herself.*

The following are ten recommendations for building a program for
preparing youth to own the Baptismal Covenant—to give one's heart to
the God of salvation recounted in the Apostle's Creed and respond by
making promises that reflect a life of discipleship.[2] For the most part,
these recommendations are practical in nature.

We begin at the beginning by wondering what your particular church
believes about the role of confirmation.

1. Discern your goals.

This might seem an obvious first step, but in the busyness of church life we
might not take the time to state our goals explicitly. Doing so will keep the
group from swimming in murky water. What do we hope to do? A natural place to look is the Baptismal Covenant. The first part—the Apostle's
Creed—recounts salvation history—what God has done, and continues to
do, for us. God created all things. God gave us God's Son who was born,
died, was resurrected, and will return. God is at work in the world today. In
the Apostle's Creed we give our hearts to the God of salvation.

The second part—the baptismal promises—is a response to God's
actions, promising to be God's people, to remain in relationship with God
and one another, and to do God's work in the world. These affirmations
and promises form, and inform, our central identity as Christians.

---

2. Using the word "preparation" is not meant to suggest that confirmation classes will culminate in
confirmation. For some it may. Others may choose not to be confirmed. Confirmation preparation is not the first of a two-part sacrament culminating in the liturgy of confirmation.

As part of the discernment process, have your church's mission statement at hand. This mission statement reflects what living the Covenant means in your *particular* location and at this *particular* time. A confirmation program in the Diocese of Arkansas whose mission statement is "We will see Jesus," for example, might emphasize looking for Jesus in very concrete places and ask candidates, "Where did you see Jesus this week?"

I asked a number of Christian educators across the country to share their goals for a confirmation program. In addition to the overarching goal of publically affirming one's faith, the most-frequently stated goals fell into five broad areas. (Each area is followed by a representative goal from a respondent.)

1. Belief

   To discuss together what we have difficulty believing, to affirm what we do believe, and raise questions that we can explore together.

2. Discipleship and ministry

   To create opportunities for confirmation candidates and sponsors to discern their own gifts and calling so that each participant gains/ deepens/renews a sense of their own unique ministry within the Church and in the world. To put the lessons into action into their daily lives.

3. Relationship

   To help [candidates] build a community of support for their journey toward deciding whether or not they want to be presented for confirmation, and potentially, to continue to support one another in their ongoing faith journeys.

4. Christian practices

   To help them discover ways to come close to the presence of God.

5. Episcopal identity

   To understand our Episcopal traditions and how our faith differs and is similar to other denominations.

What's not in this list as a goal, but is important to mention, is that nearly every respondent emphasized that confirmation is a choice for the candidate to make, not a forgone conclusion. A witness to this conviction, one congregation moderates conversations between youth who choose not to be confirmed with parents who want to "mandate" confirmation.

This list is not exhaustive. Some imply other unstated goals and each is nuanced and can be understood only in the context of how the process is lived out. Your church's goals will differ. They are presented here as examples.

Consider your goals within the context of the Christian formation programming in your church. Some of these goals are likely already being addressed in your church, which means that you might want to emphasize some goals over others. Starting at a very early age, children who have been attending have been worshiping, hearing sacred stories, wondering about meaning, developing relationships with peers and adults, engaging in service projects, forgiving, experiencing forgiveness, and reflecting theologically. By the time they enter a confirmation program, they have already been living out the Baptismal Covenant and participating in a lifelong process of transformation in Christ.

A confirmation program is part of that arc of formation. What is different is that it is an intentional time to reflect on experiences, examine beliefs, revisit sacred stories with new eyes, and discern "Do I want to give my heart to God?" "Do I want to commit to living as Christian?" and "Am I ready to do so now?" It makes sense, then, to ask where are the youth today and what formation is offered next? Simply, how does this fit into formation at our church?

Debbi Rodahaffer, Director of Christian Education at St. Matthew's in Louisville, Kentucky, shares, "We have extensive education opportunities for twos through adulthood. Most students . . . have fair knowledge of our faith, the prayer book, theology grounded in our faith before entering this [confirmation] class." At St. Paul's in Cleveland Heights, Ohio, confirmation classes are couched in a two-plus year formation program. In seventh grade, youth ask "universal questions" such as "Is there a God?" and in eighth grade explore the "so what" questions—how does faith matter? The intentional time of discerning to be confirmed occurs in the fall of ninth grade. This is the time "when it starts to 'feel real.'" The youth are also introduced to what formation program comes next. In the words of Kate Gillooly, Minister for Christian Formation and Program, "[the youth] get the message that learning is lifelong and community continues."

2. Form relationships.

Jesus begins his ministry by calling disciples—forming community. Our sacred stories are about call and response—God calls Abram, Moses, the prophets, and Mary, among many others, to relationship with God and community. In the liturgy of baptism, we answer God's call by promising to live intentionally in a community, and a confirmation program needs to model this theological understanding of living our faith.

According to Christian Smith in his book *Soul Searching*,[3] parents and "satellite" adults are two of the most important influences on the faith of teenagers. This comes as no surprise. Through actions and conversations over many years, parents play a significant role in forming a family's belief system. Parents demonstrate God's love, the character of the world in which we live, and our place in it. Satellite adults show other facets of God's love, witness to faith beyond the home, demonstrate that they are an integral part of a broader community, and are people teens can ask questions they do not feel comfortable asking their parents.

We all can name people who have influenced our lives. When I was in college I reached out to an adult friend in our church who was on the board of Planned Parenthood to ask questions I had about adult romantic relationships. These relationships showed me another facet of God's love—not better, but different. I knew our rector, John, as a friend. During confirmation classes we talked about real issues such as forgiving friends and the consequences of taking drugs. On Sunday mornings, we'd tell him jokes from *Saturday Night Live* the night before. He was a real person and showed me God's love was with me always.

Knowing that community informs the faith of all those gathered, consider the following:

- Meet with parents before the first class to describe the program and the church's expectations of parents, and to answer any questions. When we've done so at my church, the parents were better equipped to support their children along the way and understood why confirmation is a choice.
- Meet with the youth at their homes to describe what confirmation is and choose mentors together. This emphasizes that discipleship is

---

3. Christian Smith, *Soul Searching* (New York: Oxford University Press, 2009).

part of our everyday lives outside of church. Remember the first time you saw your elementary school teacher outside of class and realized they lived outside of school?

• Periodically give parents prayers their family can say together at home. Home devotions are one of the most important practices to continuing faith as an adult.

• Bless the candidates during worship as they start their journey. This acknowledges that the Holy Spirit is at work in the lives of the candidates and reminds the congregation of the promise they made at baptism to support these people in their life in Christ.[4]

• Establish and support mentor relationships. Candidates likely already have relationships with adults in the congregation whom they trust. Take the time to discern with the leadership team who has the gifts for mentoring and ask the candidates for their suggestions. Meet with the mentors as a group before the program begins and provide a framework for nurturing the mentor-candidate relationship with events and questions to discuss with their student.

3. Tell stories.

We are people of story. Through our stories we make meaning of our lives—re-telling events as we understand them, highlighting some details, and leaving others out. Hearing the stories in the Bible, we see different facets of God. By looking back on our own lives with the lens of faith, we notice God's work in ways we had not noticed before. Telling these faith stories and listening to others opens new possibilities for transformation and understanding both past and future experiences. Your confirmation program might then include:

• Reading sacred stories in the Bible. Passages to consider including are those in the Easter Vigil that recount salvation history and ask, "What does this mean to me today? What is it calling me to do?"

• Write and share your spiritual autobiographies. There are many ways to guide people in developing a spiritual autobiography. The first step is often to identify important moments in one's life and ask questions such as, "Where did I experience grace?" Godly Play offers a

---

4. See BCP 303.

particularly fun way to do so using an object box—place symbols that represent each moment in a beautiful box and take them out one by one to tell your story.

- Invite candidates to notice God during the week and share the next time you gather. One way to do this is to create a shared journal that youth can take turns bringing home. They might take pictures of where they saw God that week and place them in the journal along with a reflection.

4. Invite belief and doubt.

Paul Tillich, American theologian and philosopher, says this, "Doubt is not the opposite of faith; it is one element of faith." Doubt is what motivates questions and inquiries that lead to deeper understanding. Certainty keeps us from moving along in the journey, from responding to God's active work, and from a living relationship with God. Inviting belief and doubt has to be intentional. Ask candidates what they believe about God, Jesus, and the Holy Spirit. Ask them who and what experiences led to those beliefs. Ask trusted adults from your church who are willing to share their own questions. Explore the youth's beliefs and doubts *before* examining the Apostles' Creed; waiting until afterwards is likely to set the framework of right and wrong belief. Explore possible understandings of the Creed. What did the writers mean when they said, "born of a virgin"? Why mention Pontius Pilate? It's important to recognize that by saying this ancient creed, they join a stream of believers that reaches back to the ancient community of faith and out toward the future community. Understanding the context, the Creed and therefore one's understanding become more nuanced.

5. Engage in Christian practices.

Christian practices ground our beliefs and behavior. Prayer, silence, gratitude, reading the Bible, generosity, and observing the Sabbath build the furniture of our lives so that when the lights go out, we can still navigate the way. When we doubt, they remind us of times we believed. They orient us toward discipleship as a daily choice.

Sunday worship is our central Christian practice. It is where we are transformed week after week. Patrick Malloy, author of *Celebrating the Eucharist*, says this about worship:

The Sunday liturgy is the only time in the regular life of a community when everyone gathers. From Sunday to Sunday, individual members of the community live out their particular vocations within the baptismal vocation. On Sunday, however, the body of Christ experiences itself in its totality.[5]

The youth at Nancy Sewell's class at St. Paul's Episcopal Church in Southington, Connecticut, requires regular attendance from grades seven through ten to be eligible for confirmation. She adds, "Rarely is there a case where an exception is needed."

Rituals create holy rhythms that remind us that all time is sacred. A confirmation class might walk a labyrinth together, make Anglican prayer beads, or practice ten minutes of silence before each class. Part of a confirmation program is to provide resources for confirmands to continue to grow in faith after confirmation. Remember the maxim, "old habits are hard to break."

6. Discern ministry.

From a very young age, children are asked, "What will you do when you grow up?" Teenagers are asked, "What do you want to do after college?" (Read: What job do you want?) As a community composed of God's children, we need to get into the game, so to speak. Let youth know that what occupation they choose can be one informed by faith. It doesn't have to be becoming a priest. Jobs such as carpentry are ministry that supports living. What faith does is change our attitude of how we engage in our jobs. What ministry are you called to? By this, I mean ministry in the church and, more importantly, ministry *outside* the church.

Our baptismal promises are all about ministry in the world. We worship together to break bread and each week ask God, "Send us now into the world in peace, and grant us strength and courage to love and serve you with gladness and singleness of heart." The point is to serve God and one another—ministry.

Just like in schools where we learn what classes we do well in and what subjects we are passionate about, in church we need to engage in discerning gifts and listening for what ministry God is calling us to. For

---

5. Patrick Malloy, *Celebrating the Eucharist: A Practical Ceremonial Guide for Clergy and Other Liturgical Ministers* (New York: Church Publishing, 2007).

many youth, being called to a ministry in their daily life is a new idea. Consider using the Five Marks of Mission as a guide to identifying the variety of ministries.

7. Minister to others.

This recommendation follows up on numbers 5 and 6 above. Our baptismal promises call us outside the walls of the church to serve those who Jesus loved most—people in the periphery. Serving people identifies service as a central Christian practice. Most schools today require a certain number of hours of community service. What differentiates a service project for a confirmation class is the opportunity to reflect theologically about the work. Where is God in the community we serve? Where is God in the project? How does this work reflect on our baptismal promises? This is a good opportunity for a confirmand and mentor to work and reflect theologically together.

8. Dream a new church.

On the day we celebrate the birth of the Church (Pentecost), Peter preaches to the crowd, "In the last days, God says, I will pour out my Spirit on all people. Your sons and daughters will prophesy, your young men will see visions, your old men will dream dreams." The young *do* see visions and the old *do* dream. Give them permission to dream a new Church and share those dreams with elders in the community.

We are in the midst of a great revolution in the Church—some say as big as the Great Reformation of the sixteenth century—and, as Bishop Mark Dyer says, "we are compelled to hold a giant garage sale." Put it all out on the lawn and walk around, claim meaningful treasures and dust them off, leave what no longer speaks of the sacred in today's world.

Now, if we are to discern what to hold onto, we need to know our tradition. So take time to look at our liturgies—those in the *1979 Prayer Book* and *Enriching Our Worship*. Reflect on the mission of the Church, its polity and understanding of ministry. Then ask questions such as, "What does it mean to be the Church today?" "What words in the liturgy spark love, beauty, and transformation?" "What do we want the Church to stand for in society?" "What is enduring?" What promises does God hold for us today and the future?

Society is changing in good ways and the Church needs to change too. Young people today are digital natives that have broadened experiences and knowledge of distant worlds. The Internet has simultaneously separated and drawn people closer. Young people experience connectedness, and that worldview is affecting their choices. Take for example the emerging grace economy and the share economy.

A restaurant in Acadia National Park has no posted prices—"Pay what you can and more if you are able." After paying for the food, all the proceeds go to a local food bank. *That* is a new church. Bike-sharing has spread to many major cities, reducing consumption. *That* is a new church. Ask one another, how can we be witnesses that these are things of God? How can we, as a Church, participate in and celebrate these emerging communities? How can we see these practices as spiritual and invite others to do so as well?

As hinges between childhood and adulthood, youth are particularly poised to dream a new church into being.

The last two recommendations are simple:

9. Remember that God asks us to be faithful. God will be effective.

Confirmation is choosing a life with Christ in community. It is choosing to live as a disciple. It is a choice. Give candidates the opportunity to choose to be confirmed or not. Be sure they know that neither choice is right or wrong. This is not the only opportunity to be confirmed, and regardless of their choice, each person will continue to be part of the household of God.

Tony Pompa, Dean at the Cathedral Church of the Nativity in the Diocese of Bethlehem, asks the youth to write him a letter at the end of the final retreat. The letter is to include two things: (1) their decision about confirmation, and (2) the ministry they have discerned in the church. The first honors that confirmation is a choice. The second honors that they are an important part of the community. Not everyone will say "yes" and continue to be part of their faith community. Periodically I hear someone complaining that confirmation is a graduation ceremony. Yes, some youth do stop attending. But we do not know how God is working in their lives. In the parable of the seed growing secretly (Mark 4), Jesus tells us just that. We are asked to be faithful. God will be effective.

Lastly,

10. Return to the beginning.

Bill Lewellis, retired Canon for Communications in the Diocese of Bethlehem, writes, "One surprise after another convinces me that truth is not a thing but a *relationship* . . . and if I remain on the holy ground of relationship, born again . . . and again . . . and again . . . born from above, I remain in the story."

Let the youth know that they are writing the story of community. Let us all remain in the story.

• • •

Jenifer Lee Gamber is an author, speaker, and well-known retreat leader in the Episcopal Church. Author of the top-selling book, *My Faith, My Life: A Teen's Guide to the Episcopal Church* (Morehouse, 2006), and co-author of *Your Faith and Your Life: An Invitation to the Episcopal Church* (Morehouse, 2009) and *Call on Me: A Prayer Book for Young People* (Morehouse, 2012), she has also written leader guides for several books, including *The Heartbeat of God* by Katharine Jefferts Schori. Her website, www.myfaithmylife.org, provides numerous resources for Christian educators. She currently serves as the Director of Christian Formation at St. Anne's Episcopal Church in Trexlertown, Pennsylvania.

Jenifer acknowledges those Christian educators who offered their congregation's or diocese's practice of confirmation for this essay: Katherine Baginski Doar, Lisa Brown, Amy Cook, Randall Curtis, Laura Darling, Luke Fodor, Kate Gillooly, Carla McCook, Kim McPherson, Elizabeth Ring, Debbi Rodahaffer, Nancy Sewell, and Kellie Wilson.

CHAPTER 13

Confirmation and Catechesis

Moisés Quezada Mota

The experience I have had in the Christian formation of the candidates for Confirmation has given me the opportunity to understand how necessary it is for the Church to prepare people for catechesis and for the continuity of pastoral care for those who will be confirmed. I was confirmed at age twelve. My priest was devoted to his ministry and always tried to instruct us properly. At that time, people used the catechism from the 1928 Libro de Oración Común (LOC—Spanish translation of the Book of Common Prayer). There were twelve students, most of the same age, and we had to memorize the Creeds, the Commandments, and the major Sacraments. I think this was a custom that was traditionally practiced in the Church of that time; the belief was that we would acquire the necessary knowledge to reaffirm our baptismal vows and spiritual maturity. Unfortunately, out of the twelve candidates, only two of us remain in the Church today; the others came through the front door and then went out the back door.

It is something that is continuously repeated in many of our churches, maybe for various reasons. Some of these reasons are discussed in this material. However, I must say that it is mainly because we seldom study sacramental theology from an evangelical perspective. The sacraments in themselves are external signs with an internal spiritual grace, but they never cancel the person's initiative in his or her faith. That is why the 1979 LOC, in the catechism of the Church, calls for confirmation candidates to be instructed so they can make a mature personal decision to accept Christ as Lord and Savior. In other words, candidates must be conscious of their decision and their faith commitment.

It is for this fundamental reason that the instruction has a unique importance in the preparation of the candidates, whether they are young or old. Material that is directed to the various groups can be prepared in order to achieve appropriate formation. Educational methods can also be used for this purpose. The important thing is that the candidates for confirmation clearly internalize the process of their conversion and receive Christian formation where they can learn the fundamental beliefs of the Church, the baptismal vows, Anglican identity, and their stewardship responsibility.

Many times we do not plan confirmation classes in our annual agenda even when we know the date of the bishop's visit. We must plan ahead and include these classes in the Christian education system we have in the Church. If a Christian education program does not exist, then we must take into consideration the date and prepare a plan for confirmation classes. In both plans, within the education program or as a special program, it is essential to consider the subject matter and methodology to be used. All this can help us achieve our goal that candidates identify with the Church and know it better.

PARTICIPATION OF LAY LEADERS

In my experience as vicar of a church, I am the one doing the introduction to confirmation classes, but I always choose a layperson to be in charge of the entire program, which has been previously designed. If I am in a small church, I am in charge of teaching it and I make sure that one of the candidates teaches it in the future. This allows the preparation and participation of church leaders in the different tasks that exist in a congregation.

The preparation of lay leaders is done by diocesan programs or programs of spiritual development along with lay education in the local church. Both programs equip the laity to carry out their various ministries in the life of the Church. Many priests continue to practice clericalism by doing everything without giving broad participation to the laity. Today the idea of the entire Church being part of the priesthood has taken force, even in the Roman Catholic Church, where the laity participates actively in worship and church community activities. The laity directs the preparation of the catechumens. That is what we should do in our own churches. We must prepare them and trust their potential.

Even if one person leads the confirmation program, several laypeople can be invited to address the various topics of this program. They can also give testimony of their Christian life. In programs we have led, this lay participation has positively impacted the confirmation students. Some even remember specific moments of this experience.

A retreat can also be planned with the candidates where some church members participate in support of those who have decided to seek confirmation. "God's call" is the central theme of this retreat. We can read Bible passages of those who have received God's call. We can have a dialogue and meditate on interpretations in the context of our own journeys. All of this can be done while keeping the location and size of the congregation in mind. However, one must always think of church growth and spiritual development.

We must remember the Pauline Model that consists of establishing a church, educating the new believers, choosing natural leaders, and giving them responsibility for the new ministry. Sometimes Paul would send these natural leaders to evangelize elsewhere. This model strengthens the Church in every way. Although it may seem complicated, the model produces excellent results, as it inspires those seeking confirmation or reception to be active church members.

Whoever leads the program to prepare confirmation candidates must administer a verification test to determine the students' learning levels, and the test is modified to fit the ages and intellects of the students. This test in itself is not a requirement for confirmation or reception; it just tells us what the students have learned in the program. Almost everyone passes the test. If the group is very small, we do not administer a test.

CONTENT OF THE CLASS

The class content is paramount. To ensure an appropriate and effective program, we must choose the topics, search for available resources, and make plans, all well in advance, so the program is completely established before it even begins. Of course, all materials and plans should be in the hands of those who will teach, so they can be thoroughly prepared.

In my personal experience, I have included four aspects that I consider to be essential for a proper understanding of faith and our Church. The topics and their content emerge from these aspects.

1. The doctrine of the Church.

In the confirmation classes, we teach the essential doctrines of the Church. What do Episcopalians truly believe? What are the basic beliefs of our faith? What do Episcopalians think of the Bible, Jesus, his life, his work on the cross, his death and resurrection? These and other questions are addressed and discussed in class. The goal of this class is to get students to come to a firm conviction of their faith. They can talk with others about what they believe and so persuade those who have doubts to find the road to redemption. The doctrines of the Church, summarized in the creeds, must be explained and explored in a simple way, so they may be understood and assimilated easily. This, in turn, will dissuade members of the Church from going to other denominations.

Sadly, there are few good resources for this class since we only have the Book of Common Prayer and the Catechism found in it. The publishers that have traditionally provided Christian formation resources for our Church have provided very few materials for us to use. So many congregations turn to books from other denominations to help fill in the void.

2. The Sacraments and the Liturgy of the Church.

It is very important for the confirmation students to know that we are a liturgical and sacramental Church. We accentuate two main sacraments: Holy Baptism and the Holy Eucharist. There is a brief introduction on the Sacraments and then we go over the baptismal vows. This is a very pleasant conversation where students can speak about their own experiences and their unfamiliarity with baptism. When we have these classes, some of them even express their belief about baptism. Some believe that baptism is a type of precaution against evil spirits; others believe it is so the dead will not bother the children, and there are those who think it is only to rid their children of original sin.

The Holy Eucharist is studied through the catechism and liturgy of the Church. We teach the meaning the Church has given this sacrament as a means of grace and why it is used in different rites in the Book of Common Prayer. Depending on the group, whether it is made up of youth or adults, there is a brief overview of the three main positions historically held on the consecration of the Eucharistic elements.

Some young people complain that the Eucharist takes place every Sunday. They think it is very boring because it is so repetitive; however, when they are offered historical explanations and the intentions of the liturgy, they begin to understand more clearly the reason why each liturgical act takes place in the life of the Church. You can also involve them in the Eucharist so they can feel a sense of belonging.

Apart from the two sacraments mentioned above, the classes also talk about the five sacramental rites. The relationship between the sacraments and the spiritual life of each one of the parishioners is explored and emphasized, and educational activities regarding these sacraments take place.

The liturgical calendar or Christian year, and the symbols and meanings of the things we have on the altar are introduced. The aim is to enable the candidates for confirmation to familiarize themselves with all we use and do in the Church. All this helps the candidates know and love their Church even more.

3. History.

In this class the focus is why we are a church of Catholic tradition and what our historical heritage is. It includes the history of the beginning of Anglicanism in our country. This class is simple and interesting, as it does not dwell on dates and minute details.

Another aspect in this class is to explain a little about the Anglican Communion and how it is divided into provinces of independent churches; then there is a historical review of the Episcopal Church and its government.

4. Christian Stewardship.

This class has a particular interest because it focuses on the commitment that Christian members have for their church and community. This class is given the name "Stewardship for Life." The idea is not only economic, or only interested in offerings, but rather how God is the creator, sustainer, and merciful protector. As children of God we should cherish our lives, the lives of others, and the whole of creation. We stress being responsible and good witnesses of Christ in the world, respecting others for being made in the image of God.

Then we talk about our gratitude to God for being our creator and redeemer. We respond to this gratitude by offering our time, talent, and treasure to God. During this time we do discuss the offering and how it serves to support the work of the church and the extension of the Kingdom of God. Students are given a list of all the things the offering does in the church, from the responsibility it has with the Diocese and its missionary work, to maintenance of the property.

A sometimes very debatable point is payments received by the priest, because many come to think that all the money that enters the church also enters the priest's pocket. Obviously, this is not the case and, after sharing how the church really works in this regard, students are satisfied. I believe questions on this subject should be answered clearly in order to avoid misconceptions.

Again, the resources for each of these topics are available; all that is necessary is to organize the classes and appoint a person or a team that can present them with a clear objective.

PASTORAL FOLLOW-UP

Most of the people receiving confirmation classes are new. I say most because there are those who attend church, take communion, but do not seem interested to be confirmed or received. When this happens, talk to these people to know why they do not want to be confirmed or received. This pastoral follow-up should also be done with the candidates, but in a more direct and existential manner.

A few years ago, in a church where I was the vicar, one of the program leaders became so involved with her students that she often visited them to know how they were and to share the special moments of their lives. Her experience was such that when one of her students got into an accident and lost a lot of blood, she never left her side. The testimony was so strong that the student became a teacher in a special program the church had with street children.

This example illustrates how important it is to do pastoral work, and be present and support the candidates for confirmation. The leader should have a list of the students with their addresses and phone numbers, visit them and remember special dates, and talk with them privately. All these efforts create an atmosphere of friendship and fellowship. If it is a group of young people, having the confirmation group become part of the youth group offers the pastoral relationship. This helps in the integration of the candidates to the church.

Thus, in organizing the confirmation program, there should be a strategy for pastoral follow-up established so that the participants have a fervent testimony of God's love, and to show that the church is interested in them and their families. We must also say that the whole church as a community is called to a pastoral interrelationship.

INCLUSION

Another point to consider is inclusion. If we say that confirmation is the step for the person who is being confirmed to be part of the One, Holy, Catholic, and Apostolic Church by the laying on of the hands of the bishops, and to have the privilege to be a full member of the universal church, we must give him or her an active participation in the life of the church. In that sense the vicar or priest could discern the candidates' gifts so that when he or she deems it, they can participate in the different activities of the congregation.

Many churches ignore those who are confirmed and they remain only in the pews of the churches. Sometimes they are not assigned a specific function. There are many reasons that can range from a sense of threat from some of the church leaders to inactivity the church suffers because the vicar has little vision of his or her mission inside and outside the church.

The inclusion of the laity in general must be seen as part of the priesthood of the entire Church. The laity are not the clergy's helpers, but ministers in their own right who have answered God's call and perform their mission in the world. But this mission starts in the church community and extends where each one lives or works. The laity is then an extension of the church in the world. Upon confirmation, the candidates should be taught about this and their active participation in the various existing ministries in the community.

In addition, they should be instructed about the government of the local church and the entire Church in general, and their right to be elected and elect others. All this is part of inclusion.

There are many ministries, groups, and activities that happen in a congregation when it is not small. But even then, when a person is confirmed or received, he or she must know the organic function of the church. This process allows for the discipleship of the entire church.

This is part of my experience that I hope will be useful to many who have the task of bringing people to Christ and be members of God's body—the Church.

. . .

The Reverend Moisés Quezada Mota is the Vicar of Iglesia Jesús Naz-
areno and Rector of the school of the same name; he is also the Vicar of
Iglesia El Buen Samaritano, in San Francisco de Macorís. He was coordinator for the 9th Province and a theology professor for twenty years at
the Centro de Estudio Teológico (Center of Theological Studies) in the
Dominican Republic.

CHAPTER 14

Rites of Passage

Sharon Ely Pearson

A rite of passage is a ritual event that marks a person's transition from one status to another. Sociologically, they are often those rituals marking the transitional phase between childhood and the full inclusion of the individual into a tribe or social group. This phrase can also be used to explore and describe various other milestones in an individual's life, for any marked transitional stage, when one's social status is altered. Marriage, graduation from high school or college, and getting one's first job might be considered such a milestone.

Rites of passage have three stages: separation, transition, and reincorporation. The idea of considering Confirmation as a rite of passage or "puberty rite" has become a popular one with the rise of modern anthropology and the lack of rites for adolescents in American society. While Confirmation does not fit the criteria of a rite of passage, especially in its perpetuation of the spiritual life of the community, it is often treated as graduation from church school and/or becoming an adult in the church, rather than the beginning of a new kind of commitment.

For some, confirmation is the act that allows one to put the church behind him, knowing all "obligations" are complete, rather than as the act that initiates him into the full responsibility of living out his promises in an adult role. Even for the teen affirming these baptismal promises in good faith, there is little accountability built into the church community to help the young person keep their promises. Confirmation day is a day to dress up, become the focus of a family celebration with gifts, followed by permission to sleep in on Sunday from now on. If confirmation is by definition a time to validate, verify, make firmer, ratify, and admit the Christian into full membership (as an adult), then based on the seventy-five percent attrition rate most churches see on the Sunday after the service,[1] we have failed miserably. A Christian educator was heard saying, "We aren't confirming anything—we are hosting a charade followed by a parade—a Mass followed by a mass exodus."

Gallop polls confirm that young people begin leaving the church between the ages of twelve and sixteen,[2] and these statistics remain high.[3] Adult parish leadership and parents often state that it is natural for young people to leave the congregation and that they will return following this stage of adolescent rebellion. Assumptions like these prevent us from looking at the issues that cause young people to leave. For the most part, they are not welcome and there are no opportunities for meaningful participation. Liturgy and education programs seem irrelevant, especially if they do not apply to daily life and what is happening in the world. The Alban Institute has determined that even if teenagers have made a faith commitment to a community, they do not automatically return to the church once they've left, unless the congregation continues to extend an invitation to them between the ages of eighteen and twenty-nine when the understanding of commitment is clearer.[4] These statistics have shown that over fifty percent of those who affiliate with the Episcopal Church in adulthood do so through the ministry of higher education during the college years, showing how important delaying a commitment can be.

For most of the twentieth century, the religious and spiritual lives of adolescents were studied in order to answer the question, "How can we keep young people in church?" According to Kenda Creasy Dean, today the question is more pressing: "Does the church *matter*?"[5] Three out of four American teenagers claim to be Christian, and most are affiliated with a religious organization—but only half consider it very important, and fewer than half actually practice their faith as a regular part of their lives.[6] A number of studies[7] have shown that youth groups do important

---

1. *Confirmation as Ordination: A New FINKsperiment* (Still Waters, MN: Faith Inkubators, 2002), 9.

2. Kujawa, *Disorganized Religion*, 225.

3. A 2007 LifeWay Research study found that seventy percent of young adults who attended church in high school subsequently stopped attending church for at least a year during their college years.

4. Kujawa, *Disorganized Religion*, 225.

5. Dean, *Almost Christian*, 9.

6. Christian Smith with Melinda Lundquist Denton, *Soul Searching: The Religious and Spiritual Lives of American Teenagers* (New York: Oxford University Press, 2005), 31.

7. Three of the most encompassing studies on adolescent religiosity have been conducted by the Search Institute (*www.search-institute.org*), the National Study of Youth & Religion (*www. youthandreligion.org*), and the Exemplary Youth Ministry Study (*www.exemplarym.org*).

things for teenagers by providing moral formation, learned competencies, and social and organizational ties. But they seem less effective in providing ongoing faith formation, which is more likely to occur through their relationships with family members, mentor relationships, and congregational members who exhibit what a faithful life looks like.

As we bemoan the fact that teenagers are leaving the church, could it be that the church has abandoned them? Youth leave the church because it is solely designed to meet the needs and interests of adults, and the adults in the community are often unwilling to share their lives and faith with them. While special days may be set aside for them, such as "Youth Sundays," for many young people, they are not integrated into the life and ongoing ministry of the church, including during and after confirmation.

Often when adolescents begin to share their lack of desire to attend worship services, parents feel compelled to respond with feelings of failure and hostile compromises. Often, confirmation is used as a rite in which parents then allow their children to decide for themselves whether to attend church or not. It is assumed that their "duties" professed at each child's baptism have been completed. The promises that are made by them in the baptismal liturgy are that they bring their child up in the Christian faith and life, and that through their prayers and witness they will help their child grow into the full stature of Christ.[8] It is the entire faith community that promises to do all in their power to support each candidate in their life in Christ. Nowhere does it state that this ends at Confirmation. How does the faith community continue to be in relationship with those who have been confirmed as an adolescent?

In households where a young person's faith is nurtured in daily life, participation in the worship life of a congregation is one important aspect of faith expression. Parents often perceive that their young person is rejecting faith in God, while they are simply trying on new theologies and understandings as they begin to move from an affiliative faith to one of owned faith. Parents should be able to turn to the church for support, instead of being afraid to appear as a failure as a parent of a child who does not like church. These are opportunities for spiritual and moral guidance and support between the home and church.

Despite a desire for freedom, adolescents want limits in the form of guidelines, given with support, confidence, and affirmation. Adults need

---

8. BCP 302.

to listen and encourage adolescents to do their own believing instead of giving them faith. They do not need approval for every action, but truth and honesty that they can live with for the rest of their lives. Adults need to be continually on their own faith journey, being open to share their questions, doubts, and concerns as a fellow pilgrim on the journey. Comments such as "Church is boring!" can open a conversation around why Christians participate in communal worship, perhaps also acknowledging the need to make worship more relevant to daily life. Adults need to be clear about their own values and motivations for attending church and how they live their baptismal vows outside the church building.

Young people need guarantors or mentors, someone who is appropriately anchored in adulthood but who will walk with them on their journey. Youth advisors, teachers, clergy, relatives, and neighbors can take on the role of mentor, providing positive role models, especially if they are of the same gender, race, and ethnicity of the young person. A parish can provide such a network of mentors to assist parents in their ministry with young people.

The world and issues that confront adolescents in the United States today may not be more difficult than in previous generations, but they are different. Mass-media materialism, easy sex, violence, alcohol and drugs, and the permissiveness of individualism drive American culture. Young people make choices about their bodies and their actions, even though they lack the social and moral foundations for mature decision making in many cases.

Kenda Creasy Dean speaks of our post-modern society as pelting young people with gods from every side: good times and good looks, success and excess, health and wealth, ambition and position.[9] Our culture is full of theological images in music and movies, and theological rituals find their way into peer groups, gangs, families, and sports. Social studies discussions on freedom are theological discussions. The doctrine of creation is reflected in how we care for our environment and the treatment of gay peers. Music transports them to a mysterious higher ground, and pop stars are idols and role models. Teenagers are balancing parents, homework, careers, peers, proms, hockey, and church on the same playing field. *Rolling Stone* has observed, "Resistance is futile. Teenagers are driving our culture—and they won't be giving the keys back anytime soon."[10]

---

9. Dean, "Fessing Up," in Dean, Clark, and Rahn, eds., *Starting Right,* 29.

10. Dean, Clark, and Rahn, eds., *Starting Right,* 18.

The closest we come today in America to a rite of passage is high school, when young people begin to separate from their parents. During this time of separation, they begin to challenge the comfort of the status quo within the church and adult communities. They hang out with friends on the Internet, at coffee shops, in the mall, and at work and school. They look for mentors who are seekers of justice, and more often than not, they find these types of mentors lacking in the faith community. Questions flow easily in challenges to parents: "Why are there no black people in the congregation?" "Why are we spending $50,000 on a new organ when there are homeless on the streets?" "Why is the church not talking about human sexuality, except to argue, label, and judge?" They work hard to change a system when the system is leaving somebody out and when the system is unwilling to hear the voice of the oppressed. Too often, they are the ones who are not being heard and are being left out, and so they leave to do their ministry elsewhere.

According to the 2010 U.S. Census, there were 40,717,537 youth age 10–19 in the United States, fourteen percent of the U.S. population. And that population is also changing. In 2006, eleven percent of adolescents (ages 15–24) residing in the U.S. were born outside the United States. By 2050, the percentage of Hispanic children is expected to reach thirty-nine percent, overtaking the percentage of white-NH (thirty-eight percent) children.[11] This changing demographic is making its appearance in Episcopal churches in sacramental ways. Quinceañeras are becoming more common, as Latinos mark lavish celebrations of their daughters' fifteenth birthdays. Although the quinceañera has its emphasis on the party, it begins at the local church, where a special Mass is held in which she reaffirms her dedication to God and receives a blessing from the priest—a rite of passage marking the transition from childhood to young womanhood.

Through the *Journey to Adulthood* program, many churches have attempted to offer a rite of passage ritual to mark the movement from childhood toward adulthood. The Rite-13 Liturgy is a rite of passage where the congregation recognizes the blessing of God's gift of manhood and womanhood for those who are nearing their thirteenth birthday. The service begins with the "celebrities" sitting with their parents on one side

---

11. The Annie E. Casey Foundation, *Kids Count Working Paper* (November 2011), *http://www.aecf. org/~/media/Pubs/Initiatives/KIDS%20COUNT/T/TheChangingChildPopulationoftheUnited-States/AECFChangingChildPopulationv8web.pdf*

of the church. After receiving a blessing, they move to sit on the opposite side of the church with their older peers, symbolizing the widening world of the teenager—expanding from family influence to include the realm of peer influence. The congregation serves as an important witness to this rite. They are asked to be present with these youth through prayer and presence, being asked, "Will you, as a community of faith which spans the generations, share your knowledge, experience, and love with these young people as they begin their journey of adulthood?" The answer, similar to the reponse in our baptismal liturgy, "We will, with God's help."

If youth are the ones reaffirming their faith, it is an opportunity for the congregation to bless the growth and faith of those whom they have nurtured and provide opportunities for adults to be teachers and mentors in sharing their faith. When youth confirm their faith, they should be publicly commissioned for mission and ministry as faithful Christians in their congregation, the community, and the world. It is the action of the individual embraced and supported by the continuing action of the Spirit.

Where parish custom decrees that children in sixth grade or eighth grade or any fixed time are to "be in confirmation class," it may be impossible for those who do not feel ready to resist being confirmed along with their classmates, even if they are given a choice. This is often exhibited with the comment "everybody in my grade at church is doing it," which the church continues to promote by offering confirmation classes by grade level or age. That does not take into account the individual faith development and maturity of the individual. The flaw in this model of confirmation ministry is that it takes on the role of a rite of passage and treats the rite as a social rite. There is little connection reaffirming one's baptismal covenant with one's ongoing call to ministry, and is seen as a reward for going to all those classes, achieving an end to the education process in the church. Thus, confirmation should not be regimented by age or grade in school, but should be voluntary. It should be a sign of one's growing awareness in regard to their faith and the responsibilities that come with that recognition.

During the twentieth century a common statistic, never documented, was that eighty-five percent of commitment to Christ came before the age of eighteen. This may have been true in an earlier culture and society, but in 1999, George Barna found that only four percent of those surveyed said they had a religious conversion as a teenager. If we are confirming as a recognition of conversion and acceptance of Jesus Christ as Savior and Lord, it would seem that adolescence is not the time for asking for such a commitment while also connecting it to their rite of passage into adulthood. If adolescents are searching for their identity, we should not be encouraging them to profess a belief in anything since they are attempting to understand who they are—never mind what they believe.

In youth ministry, it is important to utilize emerging cognitive abilities as well as abstract thought in order to reflect theologically. Although developmental processes should not set the agenda for who should be confirmed, it can offer a tool to make our ministry more effective with adolescents. The emergence of formal operations leads to the idealism so characteristic of youth. We should support them in their search for identity and how faith fits into who they are. The adolescent's search for identity is ultimately a search for meaning.

When our faith communities isolate liturgy from Christian social action, young people can perceive the ritual as empty and formal. Who can take seriously a God who is detached from poverty, hunger, violence, and oppression? Liturgy can assist young people in becoming engaged in God's action in the world.

As young people work to construct a system of beliefs and values, we can provide them with many opportunities to help them consider how the faith into which we were baptized can provide the foundation for such a system. Because the process of identity formation is one that involves exploration and the trying on of roles, adults in the church must seek to balance between giving young people room to grow and experiment, and providing guidelines and expectations of what we understand ourselves to be as the church of Jesus Christ. Because they are often eager to make commitments to people, causes, ideas, and projects, but make intense commitments short term, opportunities for short-term commitments with visible exits are important. Being reprimanded for the incompletion of a long-term commitment is not supportive, and it should not be viewed as a lack of commitment, but as a developmentally appropriate action.

Instead of asking if young people are judged mature enough by the adult community, we should be asking, "What age is the most appropriate to celebrate the mutual recognition of the Spirit?" And, how can we continue to support one another in our life of faith, across all generations?

Let us acknowledge those rites of passage throughout the lifespan in appropriate ways in our congregations. Let us walk alongside our youth as they experience those milestones in their lives on their journey of faith. Let us not celebrate Confirmation as a rite of passage, but as the rite is intended to be in our prayer book—a time when an individual reaffirms their baptismal vows and recommits to a lifelong journey of faith and discernment. No matter what chronological age one is when confirmed or received in the Episcopal Church, it is a milestone event reaffirming a commitment to Christ, not a new status within the community.

· · ·

Sharon Ely Pearson was the Christian Formation Specialist with Church Publishing Incorporated from 2007–2013 before being named an editor. Prior to that she served as Children's Ministries and Christian Education Coordinator for the Diocese of Connecticut. A graduate of Virginia Theological Seminary, her thesis on *A Theology of Confirmation for the 21st Century* became the basis for new confirmation guidelines in the Diocese of Connecticut as well as several other dioceses. A noted speaker on curriculum and Christian formation, she was a member of the Standing Commission on Lifelong Christian Formation and Education during the 2009–2012 triennial and is the co-author of *The Prayer Book Guide to Christian Education, 3rd edition* (Morehouse, 2009) and *Call on Me: A Prayer Book for Young People* (Morehouse, 2012), and author of *The Episcopal Christian Educator's Handbook* (Morehouse, 2013).

CHAPTER 15

Building Base Camps

Lisa Kimball

I am generally wired for optimism, a trait that aligns well with my counter-cultural identity as a "Dream of God" Christian (think: Verna Dozier) and my passion for interpretive inquiry—wanting to understand the lived experience of human beings in their unique cultural contexts. So, while the church continues to wrestle with significant theological, liturgical, and canonical issues surrounding confirmation, I see tremendous opportunity right here, right now.

What if we were to think of confirmation as an established base camp on the Christian journey? Base camps are critical to safe climbs or treks in challenging terrain. Base camps are not the beginning of an adventurer's journey, no more than confirmation is a beginning. Base camps exist beyond the population centers (or communities) that create them. They are rustic encampments brought to life and significance by the intentions of those who pass through them. Base camps let individuals go further than they ever could alone. They are shelters and storehouses. These base camps are supplied by Sherpas, or porters, whose demonstrated gifts and wisdom support adventurers as they commit their bodies and souls to high-risk endeavor. Climbers of Mount Everest, for example, typically rest at one of the two base camps for several days to acclimatize before embarking on their climbs to the summit. When climbers' progress is threatened by inclement weather or injury, they attempt to return to the safety of base camp, ideally to venture out again a few days later. A base camp is never an end in itself. It is dependent on the resources from a source. It exists to point toward a larger reality, a sturdy way station between the known and the unknown. If confirmation is a base camp, what are the mid-journey essentials?

To understand what is essential to real-time confirmation, I asked Virginia Theological Seminary (VTS) students (by definition, anything but a random sample), "What, in your experience, is the meaning of confirmation?" I wanted to know what they understood from lived experience in the wider church, not what should be but what really is. Setting aside the predictable, disappointing responses that reflect confirmation run aground (graduation, membership credentials, social obligation, etc.), their answers begin to identify what is essential. In their words, written on newsprint in the VTS Welcome Center, confirmation is:

- A public affirmation of a personal choice to walk with Christ
- The moment I affirmed my Christian belief as an adult
- Accepting your role as a participant in the community of faith
- Being treated as a decider of one's own faith and practices
- The acceptance of my baptismal faith in front of the Body of believers and directed toward God
- Strengthening the seven-fold gifts of the Holy Spirit
- Recognition of adulthood [understood as having autonomy, agency, and responsibility] in the church
- A tangible connection to the apostolic tradition
- A rite of welcome (from another denomination)

However we choose to describe the contemporary North American religious landscape and the state of once mainline Protestant churches, study after study tell us denominational loyalty is fading, religious literacy has declined, and the number of self-identified Christians who are not confident about their beliefs is rising. Yet, despite these patterns of overall decline and drift, confirmation continues to show up in everyday life. At a minimum, parents expect it, teenagers anticipate it, and bishops value it. Confirmation lasts because human beings need sacred rituals to mark progress along the meaning-making journey that is life. In a dominant culture that too often rewards consumption and commodifies choice, the Christian journey needs established base camps where motivated individuals are welcomed, nourished, and challenged to confirm their choice of the Gospel—to become Christian disciples. What is a Christian base camp? It is a strategically planted rite along the life course. Like serious mountain climbing, religious fidelity requires decision and practice, but those virtues are individual. At a base camp the Body of Christ feeds and forms individual virtue with tradition and grace.

There are signs all around us that the Holy Spirit is working through our attempts at confirmation. Just last week, a friend who is passionate about the use of Harry Potter to teach Christian theology to youth was showing movie clips to a room full of high school sophomores. The class was made up of students from diverse racial and economic backgrounds. With the exception of two Jewish students, most had some experience of church in mainline denominations, though at different points in the course, many had stated that their families stopped attending church regularly after the children in their families reached middle school or high school.

The teacher showed a clip from the last of the eight films in the Harry Potter series. The scene showed Harry facing the brother of his hero and deceased Headmaster Albus Dumbledore. Harry has spent his entire adolescence following Dumbledore's instructions and guidance. Even after the death of Dumbledore, Harry has remained faithful to completing the seemingly impossible missions set before him by the honored great wizard. In the time Harry spends following Dumbledore's missions, many others try to convince Harry that Dumbledore is perhaps not who Harry thought he was and perhaps not someone to be trusted or followed. Even Harry's closest friends break away from him and try to persuade him that Dumbledore is not worthy of loyalty because he did not answer all the questions with which Harry and other followers of Dumbledore are left at his death.

In this intense scene, even Dumbledore's brother Aberforth lectures Harry that his famous brother is not to be trusted. And yet Harry remains faithful. Setting up the scene, the teacher said, "So Harry has to stand in front of an adult who tries to convince Harry that his, Harry's, experiences are perhaps not true or valid; that Harry's faith is misplaced and that he is perhaps too young to understand what is and what is not reality. Harry has to stand in front of that adult, and all adults like him, and declare his beliefs, whether or not anyone else agrees. . . ." One thoughtful student with bright pink hair said quietly, "So this scene is like Harry's confirmation?"

The class was silent. An ardent Harry Potter fan had taken the discussion to a new, unexpected level. She is one of the only students in the class who attends an Episcopal church regularly. The class learned that she had been confirmed the year before. To make the situation even more inspiring, the student is an emancipated minor living with a family that is not her own. Her clarity on issues of faith cannot therefore be interpreted tidily as the product of seamless adolescent development or the fruit of an intact, church-going family. In fact, she usually attends church on her own.

If a high school sophomore believes confirmation matters enough to recognize it in Harry Potter, we (the Church) have absolutely no business setting the tradition aside until we can agree on what it means. The sacrament of Confirmation brought this young woman to a place where she was able to see Harry standing at a base camp ready to name and claim the resources he would take with him. In her response to a student who asked why the situation they were watching was not baptism, the pink-haired truth-teller said, "Baptism is the beginning, and that's not what's going on. He's about to use his faith for something big: in this case to give his life for what he believes."

By grace, confirmation is a resilient, tenacious practice despite the uncertainty surrounding it. And sometimes we actually get it right. Seminarians and sophomore point toward the significance of confirmation as an existential moment, a time when their very being was recognized and affirmed for taking a stand. That moment has less to do with the ritual action of a bishop's hands and more to do with a person of any age courageously setting out to claim her place in the Christian story. As in the words of St. Paul, she is prepared to give an answer for the hope that she has.

When congregations approach confirmation assuming it has positive, lasting value, and focus on developmentally sound processes to prepare confirmands to make a decision that has real consequences, confirmation matters. When church leaders approach confirmation dismissively, apologetically, or not at all, we not only deny the promise made by every person witnessing a baptism to "do all in his or her power to support the newly baptized in their life in Christ,"[1] but we also miss a critical opportunity for Christian discipleship.

I marvel at teenagers who demonstrate their innate capacity for confirmation. In the early 1990s, I was the Coordinator for Youth and Young Adult Ministries in the Episcopal Diocese of California. I will never forget a particular Tuesday afternoon. Startled, I spun around on my office chair to see Damian and Jeff filling the entrance to my cubicle.

---

1. BCP 303.

I wasn't expecting to see them so soon. We had spent the weekend working together on the leadership team for a senior high youth event and I assumed they were back at school, back in their respective routines. Instead, I had no more than caught my breath and two 15 year old teenagers pulled up their shirts . . . I was staring at brand-new, bloody tattoos. Jeff's was on his chest, Damian's on his upper arm, but neither was pretty. What I could see, however, was that they had the same design. It was the Episcopal shield. I stuttered something like, "Tell me more. . . ." (It's important to remember that body art was not yet mainstream, not even in San Francisco!) As if rehearsed, from behind the t-shirt that was now blocking his face, Damian said, "The Episcopal Church saved my life." Twenty years later, I found Damian on Facebook and asked him about his tattoo. "I have to tell people what it is often. I tell people that it connects me to a community that I love, it is a physical reminder of a faith that was nurtured when I was a teenager and that comforts and challenges me to this day. One cannot walk around with a sign of God and not think about the responsibility to live by that covenant." I have no idea if Damian was ever confirmed by a bishop, or attends church today. What I do know is that he and Jeff created their own confirmation that Tuesday, I was privileged to be a witness, and they are still marked by it.

Think of the bold and gracious Malala Yousafzai, who is known worldwide as the famous Nobel Peace Prize runner-up for confirming her belief in the power of girls' education and non-violence in the face of Taliban threats. One year after being shot in the head by gunmen in Pakistan, on her sixteenth birthday Malala spoke eloquently to the United Nations Youth Assembly and other U.S. audiences, calling for tolerance, genuine respect for diversity, and the abolishment of all forms of discrimination based on gender. I wept the night I watched Malala on Jon Stewart, not a typical reaction to Comedy Central. Malala's resolve and fearlessness was established long before we knew her name. Who or what provided the base camp that spurred Malala to claim her place in human history?

We should not be surprised when young adults leave the church if the choices they were given were benign and did not require them to stretch. If confirmation is over after the reception, and being faithful is synonymous with being Sunday morning churchgoers, there are many more exhilarating causes to which to attach one's loyalty. Adult Christians today with no base camp will most likely not return to the beginning of their faith journey every time they need a resource. They are much more likely to stop looking that far back and join the growing population of self-identified, religious "nones." When the mission of God is reduced to select early childhood Bible stories, the vocation of God's people is stunted.

I may be optimistic, but I am not naïve. The limited data that is currently available across denominations to measure the long-term impact of confirmation on their members is not encouraging. Statistically, confirmation is more often a graduation rite and with it an exit strategy from regular involvement in the church, than it is an indicator of personal faith maturity or congregational vitality. I truly believe the discouraging findings are a reflection of how confirmation has been practiced, not a measure of its worth, and certainly not justification for its elimination. Why would an event that requires nothing more than compliance lead to lasting transformation?

The evidence that people want to confirm their faith is everywhere. Each time the church stutters or stalls surrounding confirmation practice, we let people down and obfuscate the greatest epic journey ever: Christ has died. Christ is risen! Christ will come again!

My question is whether we have the will to craft a Christian sacrament worthy of the God-given longing to commit? Can we build base camps with enough of what people need to take their faith journeys further? I pray so. They are waiting for us.

. . .

Lisa Kimball, Ph.D., is the Director of the Center for Ministry of Teaching and Professor of Christian Formation and Congregational Leadership at Virginia Theological Seminary. Her work and writing include attention to spiritual mentoring and religious identity formation in contexts of religious pluralism. Her current research includes serving as the Episcopal advisor to the Lilly Foundation-funded *Christian Youth: Learning and Living the Faith Project,* which seeks to learn the extent to which confirmation and equivalent practices in five Protestant denominations in North America are effective for strengthening discipleship in youth.

PART IV

A THEOLOGY OF CONFIRMATION FOR THE FUTURE

I pray that, according to the riches of his glory, he may grant that you may be strengthened in your inner being with power through his Spirit, and that Christ may dwell in your hearts through faith, as you are being rooted and grounded in love. I pray that you may have the power to comprehend, with all the saints, what is the breadth and length and height and depth, and to know the love of Christ that surpasses knowledge, so that you may be filled with all the fullness of God. Now to him who by the power at work within us is able to accomplish abundantly far more than all we can ask or imagine, to him be glory in the church and in Christ Jesus to all generations, forever and ever. Amen.

—Ephesians 3:16–20

CHAPTER 16

Lifelong Christian Formation

The Episcopal Church carries out God's mission through the ministry of all its members, which is dependent on the formation and education of all ages—children (0–12), youth (13–18), young adults (18–35), adults (over 35), and older adults. This is a lifelong journey, requiring a multitude of opportunities for learning and reflection. At the 77th General Convention in 2009, *The Charter for Lifelong Christian Formation* was adopted. It states that Christian education and formation is foundational to all that the Episcopal Church does—on the local, diocesan, and church-wide level. As the Charter states, "Christian Formation in the Episcopal Church is lifelong growth in the knowledge, service and love of God as followers of Christ and is informed by Scripture, Tradition and Reason."[1] For the Church to pass along the faith to future generations, its members must be equipped to experience, proclaim, and invite others to share the Good News. Our baptismal promises commend us to continue in the apostles' teaching and fellowship, in the breaking of the bread, and in the prayers. We are continually being formed as Christians by being equipped to proclaim the Gospel, offering service to others, advocating for justice and peace, and respecting all persons. It is a lifelong journey.

The Book of Occasional Services 2003 offers a process for those reaffirming baptismal vows. The methodology of learning is not the classroom model where one passes the course and is confirmed; rather, it is a formative process. It is a series of rites and stages that employs a process similar to that of the catechumenate to prepare mature baptized persons to reaffirm their Baptismal Covenant and who wish to receive the laying on of hands by the bishop.

---

1. *http://formationcharter.com*

Stage Two. This is a longer period during which those being formed, along with sponsors, catechists, and other members of the community engage in deeper exploration of faith and ministry.

This formation period is based on a pattern of experience followed by reflection. The baptized persons explore the meanings of baptism and the baptismal covenant, while discerning the type of service to which God calls them in the context of the local community. The sponsors and catechists in turn train and support them in that service and help them to reflect theologically on their experience of ministry through the study of Scripture, in prayer, and in worship. Substantial periods of time are spent doing ministry and reflecting on it with catechists and sponsors.[2]

A final period after the third rite leads to the Reaffirmation of the Baptismal Covenant at the Easter Vigil and the presentation of the candidate to the bishop for Confirmation, Reception, or Commitment to Christian Service during the Great Fifty Days of Easter. Throughout, the candidate is lifted up in the faith community as a living example of our common need to continually examine our lives in terms of our baptismal promises. This authorized rite should be used annually in parishes, with diocesan training for its implementation if necessary.

Christian education is only one component of a church's ministry. It is inseparable from congregational life, especially its worship. Also, what is done in the church must be supported in the home. There has to be a connection to ministry and mission in the classroom, church, and greater community. Most Christian education continues to be segregated for children in Church School and those involved in Confirmation/Reaffirmation programs. Creating curricular resources, training teachers, and holding classes and activities for children and youth without changing the congregational system will continue to undercut the ongoing spiritual formation of our youngest members. We need to find ways in which a congregation will call and support all members, no matter their age, to individual ministry—then provide support for them as they live out their call.

Whenever a bishop visits a congregation, there should be a renewal of baptismal vows by all present. There is a collegial relationship between the bishop and the congregation and their mutually reinforcing participation

---

2. *The Book of Occasional Services 2003*, 137.

in apostolic ministry. The church, as well as the individual, is blessed by the apostolic authority of a bishop that is given to him or her by the apostolic authority of the Church at their consecration. The bishop should also take the opportunity to meet with children, youth, and adults for conversation if at all possible. This will mean planning and coordination between the parish liturgy committee, church school volunteers, and youth leadership—a wonderful practice to have on a continuing basis to ensure the involvement of all ages in the worshipping life of a community. Rites of transition that mark milestones in people's lives should be celebrated, with rituals written by the community for such times as acquiring a driver's license, graduation from high school, entering college or the world of employment, serving in the military, the adoption of a child.[3]

Congregations need to keep in contact with young people as they go off to college or other pursuits. Maintaining a relationship of care and support at a distance will show the true nature of what a caring community is all about. As young adults continue independent living, their faith is challenged and they begin to explore life for themselves, many for the first time in their lives.

Resolutions that came before the 78th General Convention in 2012 that proposed amending the Constitution and Canons regarding the requirement of being confirmed to hold a leadership position in the Episcopal Church do not detract from the importance of lifelong formation, but address an ongoing need of formation: that people in leadership positions in the Episcopal Church, such as members of a vestry, delegates to diocesan convention, and other appointive or elective positions, demonstrate adequate formation in Episcopal identity. It is important to form new members and those elected to leadership positions in Episcopal identity and governance, building upon the foundation of baptismal catechesis and lifelong learning opportunities for all members. However, baptism equals full membership, so confirmation should not be a prerequisite for leadership. Continuing formation—yes.

Spiritual formation is not simply an internal process, but is an ongoing engagement with a community of faith. While spirituality is often perceived as an individual experience, it has a social dimension. It is a

---

3. *Changes: Prayers and Services Honoring Rites and Passages* (New York: Church Publishing, 2007) is a collection of prayers and rites developed for use in the Episcopal Church by the Standing Commission on Liturgy and Music for congregations, families, and individuals.

community of faith. Formalized faith begins when one internalizes the content and practices of their faith community, accepting and adapting them to their own understanding of and relationship to God. A new practice of ongoing reaffirmation should be rooted in our understanding of the historic unity of baptism, confirmation, and communion. It should be a repeatable rite of the church in which members say "yes" to their baptism by acknowledging faith-strengthening experiences throughout the course of their lives. The church should encourage and provide all its members with opportunities for continuing to form their faith through experiences of witness, service, worship, and education.

CHAPTER 17

A Proposed Theology

It can be said that the Church in the late twentieth century began a shift from Christendom to a post-Christian era. Today's Church finds itself in a very similar circumstance as the early Church found itself—small communities following the teachings of Jesus Christ living in a world that does not share the same ethos and vision of God. An individualistic society, we make our own decisions as to whether we practice any faith, let alone participate in a faith community on a regular basis or adhere to any creed, doctrine, or denominational tradition.

In the Episcopal Church, baptism is full incorporation into a faith community that stands apart from secular society. In the days of Tertullian and Hippolytus, the Church had no rite called Confirmation. The sealing with chrism and the hand-laying were integral parts of the baptismal rite. These acts were closely associated with the giving of the Holy Spirit, which was why a bishop was its administrator. Today, Baptism necessitates a depth of commitment by parents and sponsors who bring infants and children to the font, where before it had been adults who made such a commitment for themselves (and their households).

Besides differing views on scriptural evidence, the best way to determine a theology of confirmation is to view early liturgical practice as a primary source. It was formative of Christian theological thought before the New Testament documents were canonized, and the comments of early Christian writers are just as appropriate today in a post-Christian era as they were in a pre-Constantine era. Today, it is imperative that lifelong formation be recognized and parishes focus on the catechesis and preparation of parents prior to baptism. The church should be giving support to adults in their new role of parenthood in bringing up their children in a life of faith. God is moving in history to challenge, demand, call, and open us up to new possibilities for birth in the world. Baptismal assumptions, practices, and understandings of confirmation from a Christendom point of view in this post-Christian era will undermine the role that the adolescent can play in the Church of today and tomorrow. As a faith community, we need to know our own calling so that we can be effective in ministering with our teenagers, modeling to them an effective way of living in today's society. We must continue to question and reevaluate; the Church is very much an adolescent itself, still seeking to find out its role in God's creation.

Kenda Creasy Dean states the issue we are faced with:

> Overall, the challenge posed to the church by the teenagers in the National Study of Youth and Religion is as much *theological* as methodological: the hot lava core of Christianity—the story of God's courtship with us through Jesus Christ, of God's suffering love through salvation history and especially through Christ's death and resurrection, and of God's continued involvement in the world through the Holy Spirit—has been muted in many congregations, replaced by an ecclesial complacency that convinces youth and parents alike that not much is at stake. In the view of American teenagers, God is more object than subject, an Idea but not a companion. The problem does not seem that churches are teaching young people badly, but that we are doing an exceedingly good job of teaching youth what we really believe: namely, that Christianity is not a big deal, that God requires little, and the church is a helpful social institution filled with nice people focused primarily on "folks like us"—which, of course, begs the question of whether we are really the church at all.[1]

Urban Holmes once said that confirmation is "rather like Humpty Dumpty, and that we could not simply reverse history and put the pieces back together again."[2] We must continue to live in the tension of the concluding (*missa*) episcopal rite of the early Church's integrated pattern and the Reformation's rite of owning of the faith by someone who had been baptized as a child and who had now reached "maturity." Becoming a mature Christian is always a demand, a challenge, and an opportunity. The process of maturity is always in relation to a particular circumstance

---

1. Dean, *Almost Christian*, 11–12.

2. Weil, "American Perspectives: (ii) Confirmation," 72.

and situation. In confirmation, the situation is in the church in relation to society. As the society has changed, the ritual and catechetical measures that may have signified maturation in the past now seem inappropriate.

What does "mature'" mean today? It does not need to be associated with age. Maturity can be measured in a willingness of engagement in conversation about faith, and the ability to articulate what one believes in relationship to ministry in the world. Above all, it is an understanding of what it means to make a commitment to continue in the apostles' teaching and fellowship, in the breaking of bread, and the prayers. It means being able to proclaim by word and example the Good News of God and Christ, seeking and serving Christ in all persons, and striving for justice and peace among all people. As the Right Reverend James E. Curry, Bishop Suffragan of Connecticut, states using the words of Roland Allen, it is being able to "pray the prayer of Christ, know the mind of Christ, and do the deeds of Christ." Being "duly prepared" means being engaged in heart and mind to be ready to voluntarily profess one's faith. We cannot be indoctrinated into a mature commitment to Christ; it is a continual process of formation in which we are appreciative of the mystery and reverence of our life and the life of Jesus Christ.

While there are many moments in a person's life when the Holy Spirit comes, there is a special moment when one desires to make a personal commitment in a public assembly to follow Jesus Christ as Lord and Savior for the first time. It can be a powerful moment of invocation of the Spirit, acknowledging its continuing power and mystery that is continually working in our lives. The Episcopal Church can embrace its tradition of apostolic succession by continuing to recognize one's Reaffirmation when confessed in the context of the greater Christian community, celebrating the life that God gives freely and supported in community. Just as a bishop and priest have received the laying on of hands in apostolic succession, every Christian can claim ordination to the ministry of all the baptized.

Both baptism and confirmation are the means and occasions for response to grace and the gift of the Holy Spirit. By baptism we are made full members in the Body of Christ, and in it we are sealed and confirmed as Christ's own forever. The rite of Confirmation should be truly recognized (in title) as a rite of reaffirmation to include the laying on of hands by a bishop that represents the continuing work of the Spirit in a person's life while also connecting the person to the wider apostolic community. The act of reaffirmation is a conscious decision on the part of a person to not be recognized as an adult in the faith community, but as an ambassador for Christ. Preceding and following such a reaffirmation, opportunities for personal instruction and community building should be provided on a parish and diocesan level.

Baptism preparation should be essential and ongoing, with the faith community supportive of families who desire to have a child baptized. The obligation of parents and godparents should be seen as one of nurture and partnership on the journey, with a supportive faith community always present. Congregations need to take seriously the promises they make at baptisms, and be held accountable for their embracing and nurture of all children and youth in the congregation. Understanding Christian formation as a lifelong journey for all will open up the recognition of God working in everyone's life. Such environments of hospitality and safety will provide opportunities for individuals to explore and confess their own faith, independently of peers, parents, and culture.

Ministry with young people needs to include diverse models of learning and a connection with the congregation in its life of worship, identity, mission, discipleship, and vocation. Adult involvement in education and service will provide models of living out our baptismal promises. Youth are helped to mature in faithfulness through learning with peers and persons of all ages and cultures, including teachers, mentors, priests, parents, and bishops. For such learning to take place, congregations need to be hospitable places for youth. A faith community can accept their gifts, questions, struggles, and energy by inviting them to share their ideas and willingness to participate. Risk is involved, but that is where transcendence occurs.

Congregational reaffirmation ministry needs to be Gospel centered and open to the grace of God, whether it is in content-centered programs or acting out the mission of the church. Churches can develop "reaffirmation ministry teams" to give shape to the pastoral and educational components for ministry with middle and high school students. The outcomes of these programs should not lead to reaffirmation (confirmation), but provide ongoing opportunities for young people to explore their articulation of their faith. Dioceses, seminaries, and the church-wide bodies can be in partnership with congregations in providing support resources, such as materials, networks, and leadership. Opportunities for all ages to engage in the biblical story while engaging in Gospel-based ministry in the local community are critical elements to assist people of all ages in articulating their faith.

What if the season of Lent became a time when the entire Episcopal Church prepared for the Pascal mystery while reliving our salvation story and discernment of how we live out our call in the world? For youth, deanery or convocational events can bring congregations together for sharing, fun, mutual learning, and an understanding of the diversity of the diocese and Church. Retreats or "Bishop's Days" can be held for young people to meet with the bishop, learning about his or her role in the Church and their understanding of how God acts in their life and the role of Jesus Christ in their ministry in the world. During the Easter season, regional celebrations in a diocese could be held, inviting all who wish to personally receive a blessing (in the form of laying on of hands) and strengthening of the Spirit from the bishop.

When a bishop visits a congregation, baptisms should be celebrated, with the laying on of hands as part of baptism. The entire congregation can be invited to reaffirm their baptismal promises, with a catechumenal period for all prior to his or her visitation. Those who feel so called and prepared, can come forward to receive the laying on of hands in reaffirming their baptism in the midst of their community of support. Youth will not accept adult responsibilities if they see the adults around them refusing to accept their own responsibilities: adults who do not attend worship regularly, who moan about their pledges and the church budget, who complain about parish or diocesan politics, who do not live out the Gospel in their daily life.

We should focus on *The Reaffirmation of Baptismal Vows*, which is what our rite of Confirmation really is, acknowledging that confirmation occurs at the signing and dismissal from Holy Baptism. Unified rites of baptism, confirmation, and holy communion can inspire Christians to live with the tension between day-to-day life in a secular culture and the vision of faith taught by the early Church.

No matter what age, a congregation needs to embrace and fully include the young people just as any other adult member. This means being able to serve at the altar, on a vestry or search committee, or any other parish committee, whether "confirmed" in today's sense or not. Their voices should be encouraged to be heard as part of any parish planning decision and be given responsibility (with adult mentorship and support) to live out those tasks. Recognition of their individual gifts and providing opportunities for them to share in ministry can help incorporate them in the post-confirmation period, assuming the role of adulthood.

It is time to lift up the centrality of baptism as full membership in Christ's Church. A rite of re-commitment with regular dedication to discipleship, service, and mission as expressed every time we celebrate Holy Baptism should be emphasized. Mature members of the faith community should be engaged in learning contexts with younger members. Congregations need to be catechumenal communities, focused on the ministry of all the baptized, accepting the gifts of all ages.

The 2009 General Convention adopted *The Charter for Lifelong Christian Formation*, which describes the many processes by which we live into our Baptismal Covenant. The explanation accompanying that resolution explained the vision underlying the Charter in this way: "We affirm that lifelong Christian formation is foundational to the success of any church, and in the case of our own, is an integral part of the process by which we will rebuild the Episcopal Church. Our congregations will grow in numbers and health when they are supported by leaders—of all orders of ministry—who know their identity in Christ and are able to access their tradition for the purposes of proclaiming and living out the Gospel."[3]

Throughout our biblical tradition we are told the stories of God's people responding to God's call. Abraham's response to the angel of the Lord: "Here I am" (Gen 22:11). Moses' response to God in the burning bush, "Here I am" (Ex 3:4). Samuel finally realizes that it was the Lord calling him, "Here I am" (1 Sam 3:8). Isaiah responds to the word of God, "Here am I; send me!" (Isa 6:8). Mary responds to the astounding news of the angel Gabriel, "Here am I, the servant of the Lord; let it be with me according to your word" (Lk 1:38). And Acts 9:10 shares the story of Ananias, a disciple in Damascus who responds to a vision with, "Here I am, Lord." The rite of Confirmation gives an individual the opportunity to say, "Here I am Lord."

In baptism we have been sealed by the Holy Spirit and marked as Christ's own forever. With God's help we have been "signed, sealed, and delivered." Our response to God when we reaffirm our baptismal promises is, "Here I am Lord—I'm yours!"

---

3. *Report to the 77th General Convention* (otherwise known as the Blue Book), 153–154.

Discussion Guide

The meaning of confirmation in the Episcopal Church today varies depending on one's personal experience, knowledge of the history of the practice of confirmation, and understanding the role that baptism plays in the church's polity.

The following discussion questions offer a process for gathering individuals together to discuss what confirmation means to them in light of their own experience. Particular audiences in addition to those adults who simply wish to study and learn about the role of confirmation in the Episcopal Church might include parents of young people who are preparing for the rite of Confirmation, especially if they are new to the Episcopal Church or were confirmed themselves prior to 1979 when the 1928 Book of Common Prayer was used and when confirmation was needed in order to receive Holy Communion. Another audience might be those who seek to understand the baptismal ecclesiology of the 1979 Book of Common Prayer more fully. As General Convention continues to put forth resolutions regarding confirmation as needed for leadership in the Episcopal Church as stated in the Constitution and Canons, hopefully this will also be a source for conversation before deliberations.

1. What was your confirmation experience?

   - How old were you?
   - Where were you living?
   - What church or denomination were you part of?
   - What did your preparation entail?
   - How did your experience prepare you to renew your commitment to Christ?
   - In retrospect, what could have been different?

2. What vows have you made in your life? How well have you kept them? What or who helped you sustain and nurture those promises over the years?

3. What do you believe is the purpose of confirmation?

   • What do you believe the effects of confirmation are, if any?
   • What is the view of confirmation in your congregation?

     ◦ Parents
     ◦ Young people
     ◦ The congregation in general

4. There are two prayer "options" (BCP 309) to be said at the laying on of hands: "*Strengthen, O Lord . . .*" and "*Defend, O Lord. . . .*" If either, which do you prefer, and why?

5. Would you describe confirmation as sealing or strengthening? Why?

6. "*In the course of their Christian development, those baptized at an early age are expected, when they are ready and have been duly prepared, to make a mature public affirmation of their faith and commitment to the responsibilities of their Baptism and to receive the laying on of hands by the bishop.*" (BCP 412)

   • What do you believe is meant by "duly prepared"?
   • What do you believe is meant by "mature" affirmation and commitment?

7. What do you believe is the difference between the gift of the Spirit at Baptism and the gift of the Spirit at Confirmation?

8. How important is the imposing of hands for the administration of Confirmation?

9. At what age (if you believe in a "minimum") should Confirmation be held, and why? If you do not believe there should be a "minimum," why?

10. What elements should be part of a substantive faith-formation experience for youth who are preparing for confirmation? Adults?

11. Does your diocese have standards or guidelines for confirmation? If so, when and how were they developed, and what do they include?

12. More and more dioceses are holding "regional" Confirmation services as opposed to local parish rites. How do you feel this supports (or detracts) from your view of confirmation?

13. If describing Confirmation as a specific type of rite, would you describe it as a rite of intensification, community, transition, or initiation? Why?

14. What difference does your faith make in your life? How does your belief in God affect the way you live, the decisions you make, the relationships you have with others? What aspects of your life do you keep separate from your faith? Why?

15. What does it mean to accept Jesus Christ as your Savior and Lord?

If using this book for adult study and reflection, the following questions may add to your group conversation for each chapter:

1. *Rites of Initiation in Christian Tradition*: Read Acts 8:4–25, Acts 19:1–7, 2 Cor 1:12–23, and pages 306–308 in the Book of Common Prayer (Thanksgiving over the Water). What is the action of the Holy Spirit? How has the rite of Confirmation grown out of these parts of our tradition?

2. *Liturgical Renewal of Christian Initiation Rites*: How is Confirmation a pastoral rite? How does it now relate to baptism?

3. *Christian Initiation and the Adolescent*: What is your understanding of adolescence? Do you feel confirmation (or reaffirmation) is appropriate for this age? Why or why not?

4. *The Catechumenate*: If you were to prepare for and plan your baptism now, what would that "catechumenal process" look like? What would the liturgy be like? What symbols of baptismal faith and new life would you include?

5. *Re-Imagining Confirmation*: The Reverend Dr. Ruth Meyers emphasizes, "Confirmation, then, is *not* a rite of Christian initiation, incorporating believers into the body of Christ. In the 1979 BCP, confirmation is a rite of renewal and reaffirmation, a part of Christian life rather than the completion of initiation into that life." What is your understanding of the difference between confirmation, reaffirmation, and reception? What do you believe the role of the bishop should be in each circumstance? What preparation is needed for each?

6. *A Liturgy for the Messy Middle*: Are we in a post-confirmation church? What do you believe needs to change? Of the recommendations made by Bishop Mathes, which do you agree with, and why?

7. *A Rite in Search for a Reason of Being*: What are the pastoral implications of offering confirmation? Are there pastoral implications for not making this rite regularly available in a congregation?

8. *Contemplating Our "One Wild and Precious life"*: Contemplate your "one wild and precious life." Where and when has your life seemed to have been most in tune with those vows, and where and when not and why? How do these vows make sense in the mystery of your life that is still undiscovered territory?

9. *Confirmation and Sacraments in Latino Ministries*: How is your congregation open and inclusive to the needs of Latinos in your community? How can we (Anglos and Latinos) celebrate the spirituality found in the Episcopal Church's understanding of the sacraments?

10. *Christian Identity*: Bishop Singh states, "The call for Christian leadership is about clarifying one's identity as a child of God and one's vulnerability in seeking reconciliation with other people, creation, and all manner of life." How do you live this out in your life as a Christian? Does one's preparation for confirmation inform this call? If so, how?

11. *Everything You Need to Know To Be Confirmed*: What do you believe it means to be "duly prepared" for confirmation? What would you add or detract from Reverend Darling's considerations on how we approach confirmation preparation?

12. *Practical Matters*: How was your choice of being baptized and confirmed similar or different than Ms. Gamber's? What goals does your congregation have in planning confirmation preparation?

13. *Confirmation Preparation*: What are ways we can strengthen our teaching practices, content offered, and pastoral responses in preparing confirmands?

14. *Rites of Passage*: How can the Episcopal Church institute formal rites of passage, allowing the rite of Confirmation to be a reaffirmation of baptism? What recognition (and inclusion) do young people seek in your congregation?

15. *Building Base Camps*: Dr. Kimball states, "What is a Christian base camp? It is a strategically planted rite along the life course. Like serious mountain climbing, religious fidelity requires decision and practice, but those virtues are individual. At a base camp the Body

of Christ feeds and forms individual virtue with tradition and grace."
What does it take to have confirmation become an existential moment
for an individual? How can the church become a base camp providing
an environment that feeds and forms?

16. *Lifelong Christian Formation*: Read *The Charter for Lifelong Christian
    Formation*, *http://formationcharter.com*. What word or phrase stands
    out to you? What is going on in your church that is a good example
    of this? What might the Charter be calling your church to do? What
    part of the Charter draws your own energy?

17. *A Proposed Theology*: Read the two Episcopal News Service stories
    found in Appendix I. How do you respond to the questions asked in
    these stories? What is YOUR theology about confirmation?

News Articles

November 9, 1977

Liturgical Commission Issues "First Communion" Statement[1]

Episcopal News Service

DALLAS, Tex.—No special form for the admission of baptized children to Holy Communion is desirable, the Standing Liturgical Commission declared in a statement adopted unanimously at its meeting in mid-October.

Meeting at the Center for Continuing Education of St. Matthew's Cathedral here, the Commission, one of the Standing Commissions of the Episcopal Church's General Convention, considered this question along with other matters arising from the preparation of a Book of Occasional Services.

The Commission recognized the uneasiness that many people feel concerning the reception of Communion by small children, but concluded nevertheless that the provision of officially authorized forms for admission to Communion "would obscure the principle that Holy Baptism is full initiation by water and the Holy Spirit."

It warned against the adoption of "certain artificial norms," such as the arbitrary setting of a fixed age for "First Communion"; the introduction of children to the Sacrament in a context that separates them from their own families; and the temptation to form "First Communion classes" on the model of confirmation classes.

The Commission commended the practice of admitting individual children to regular reception of Communion upon evidence of their desire to communicate, and after consultation between the parish priest and the parents. "Practical efforts to enhance the sense that baptized children are, in fact, full Christians are to be commended and encouraged," the Commission concluded.

Should confirmation be required?[2]

By Pat McCaughan

August 28, 2012

[Episcopal News Service] When the Reverend Canon Lee Alison Crawford told vestry members church canons required they be confirmed, an anguished junior warden resigned.

"As the (former) rector of a congregation whose average Sunday attendance was under 50, which gave me a core group of maybe 30 people, I usually found out by accident that somebody hadn't been confirmed," recalled Crawford, during a recent telephone interview.

She refused his resignation. "I said to him, you are one of the most faithful people I know. You already have a leadership position. You understand the church. In a small congregation I would say confirmation for leadership is an ideal but in theory and practice it doesn't always happen," said Crawford, a General Convention deputy from Vermont.

---

1. *http://www.episcopalarchives.org/cgi-bin/ENS/ENSpress_release.pl?pr_number=77368*

2. *http://episcopaldigitalnetwork.com/ens/2012/08/28/should-confirmation-be-required/*

"With the change in theology in the 1979 prayer book, with baptism the root of everything we do, confirmation is a rite looking for a theology," she added.

The confirmation requirement for leadership was the subject of intense conversation but not much consensus at the 77th General Convention in Indianapolis, said Deborah Stokes, a lay deputy from the Diocese of Southern Ohio.

Ultimately, General Convention rejected or referred for further conversation several resolutions proposing removal (A042, A043) or review (A044) of confirmation as a requirement for church leadership.

"We felt very strongly this was just the beginning of the conversation," said Stokes, co-chair of the legislative committee on education, which considered the resolutions. "I didn't want to lose confirmation, and I think all of us feared losing it if it's not a requirement for something."

Rather than eliminate it the proposed changes intended "to free confirmation to be a response to baptism, a pastoral response that might occur in various ways in people's lives," said the Reverend Ruth Meyers. The Hodges-Haynes Professor of Liturgics at the Church Divinity School of the Pacific, she consulted with the Standing Commission on Lifelong Christian Formation (SCLCF), which authored the resolutions.

She was surprised by the reaction to the proposed changes. "People had the sense that, by taking it out of the canons, we were wanting to do away with confirmation. That's absolutely not the case."

Rather, the canonical changes were intended to offer options. "We could just say that baptism, with some instruction in the history and governance of the church, is really what you need for leadership" allowing confirmation to follow "as a response to baptism at a time that makes sense to you."

Bishop Porter Taylor of Western North Carolina, SCLCF vice chair, said the changes would make the rite more a response to the movement of the Holy Spirit and less "a hoop that we have to jump through. We don't see confirmation as part of our governance."

"And this is not about saying I want to be a member of the Episcopal Church," he said during a recent telephone interview. "This is about saying that God has been doing something in my life and I want to mark that by standing up in the midst of the congregation and having the bishop lay hands on me in order to mark the movement of the Holy Spirit."

For Lillian Sauceda-Whitney, who was confirmed May 6 at St. Margaret of Scotland Church in San Juan Capistrano, California, confirmation felt like "I had finally found my home. It was like being baptized."

Bishop Stacy Sauls, chief operating officer of the Episcopal Church, confirmed the 59-year-old preschool teacher and more than a dozen others on behalf of Bishop Jon Bruno of Los Angeles.

"I had tears of joy," Sauceda-Whitney recalled during an Aug. 23 telephone interview. "I really wanted to belong. I thought, it's time for me to stand up and say I am an Episcopalian. I thought the only way to do that would be to join the church."

Whether confirmation is required of church members in general and leaders in particular since it is no longer needed to receive communion, is a conversation that needs to happen organically, at all levels of the church, especially in the parish, said the Reverend Elizabeth Kaeton, a retired priest in the Diocese of Newark.

"It's about belonging," Kaeton said during a recent telephone interview. "I think we're still not clear in our society and that's reflected in our church, about what it means to belong. In the church we're trying to figure out what it means to be an Episcopalian. We're also struggling with what does it mean to have a public profession of faith."

"Rather than being tied to a rite of passage or an age, confirmation should be linked to a process of Christian formation," she said. "It's an exciting conversation. We've stopped talking about sex and now we're talking about money and baptism and confirmation and marriage and these are important things."

Another education committee member, the Reverend Charles Holt, rector of St. Peter's Church in Lake Mary, in central Florida, said he was relieved and grateful that "none of the resolutions passed General Convention."

Had they passed, theoretically, "all one had to do to be an elected leader at the highest levels was to have taken communion three times over the course of last year" or be a communicant in good standing, he said. "Conceivably, they could not believe in Jesus Christ as their Lord and personal savior and be a leader in the Episcopal Church."

The conversation about confirmation is essential and a healthy one because "it makes us recommit ourselves and come to clarity about our core beliefs and wrestle with our faith," said Holt.

Holt also believes confirmation "is actually the one thing a bishop can do to help grow the Episcopal Church. In the Episcopal Church, it's the bishop's job to make sure that every single person who's a member of our church has made a mature profession of faith in Jesus Christ"—a moment he believes every Christian should experience.

"If we do away with confirmation then we don't have that moment for people," he said.

Making confirmation a powerful and personal moment is of utmost importance for Bishop Dorsey Henderson, who retired from the Diocese of Upper South Carolina in 2009. He now assists on behalf of Bishop Gregory Brewer of Central Florida at confirmations.

Henderson confirmed about 18 people at St. Peter's Church on May 17, including eighth grader Grant Williams, 13, who believes "confirmation is very necessary.

"It felt like I was coming closer to God, like I was getting to know him better and confirming my faith in him by showing that I truly believed in him and wanted to follow him," he said.

Henderson said he adds the names of each confirmand to a personal notebook he has kept over 15 years of the episcopacy. "I assure them that I will pray for them regularly by name and I ask them for their prayers."

While confirmation "is not essential to receive the sacrament of Holy Communion . . . it provides a kind of spiritual boost" especially to those baptized as infants and those converting from other traditions, he said during a recent telephone interview.

Bishop Dan Martins of the Diocese of Springfield, said confirmation evolved the way it did because of practical necessity—because dioceses grew and "bishops could not multi-locate."

What began as one service including baptism followed with laying on of hands by the bishop and a prayer for the gifts of the Holy Spirit over time "was separated and priests were authorized to celebrate at the water portion, with the understanding that at some point they would bring the newly baptized to the bishop for the laying on of hands. Eventually it took on a life of its own as a separate event and acquired the name confirmation," he said during a recent telephone interview.

The rite may evolve, but bishops remain a symbol "of the wider church, our organic connection to church through time and space," he added. "The prayer may change, the name we use is in flux, but . . . as the sacramental sign of ministry, then it's important that everybody come under the hands of the bishop at some point in their public profession of Christian faith and discipleship."

The Reverend Tom Woodward, a retired priest residing in New Mexico and a long-time General Convention deputy, believes baptism and confirmation should both be delayed, to about 16 and 26 respectively, to allow for more mature professions of faith.

"A child in middle school or high school who's being baptized—his or her friends would come to that service and it's a powerful witness of the decision to be baptized," he said during a recent telephone interview. "Confirmation class would include a discernment of ministry and gifts, Then, when the bishop comes to invoke the Holy Spirit it would be very similar to the ordination process, adding to the dignity and power of commission of lay ministry in the world."

Timing had everything to do with confirmation for Karen Lander, 45, and Henry Lutz, 14, also confirmed May 6 at St. Margaret's in San Juan Capistrano by Sauls.

"I decided since I was sending my eight-year-old to her first communion classes, it was time for me to do my confirmation as well," Lander said during a recent telephone interview. "I have to be an example to her. I needed to learn more about the church instead of just going to church." For Lutz, who is entering the ninth grade this year, it was a communal experience. "The bishop put his hands on me, and the priests and my family did the same.

"I gained a wisdom through the whole experience. I understand what I'm doing with the Bible, what I can interpret from God and so many parts of the Episcopal Church. I interpreted it as a sign of how I'm taking my faith to a different path now, knowing that I'm getting a stronger faith and ready to do more."

Annotated Bibliography of Confirmation Resources

A People Called Episcopalians: A Brief Introduction to Our Peculiar Way of Life by John H. Westerhoff (Morehouse Publishing, 2002)—A forty-page booklet that attempts to address the foundational issues of what it means to be an Episcopalian, devoting chapters to things Anglican: Identity, Authority, Spirituality, Temperament, and Polity. For adults.

Confirm not Conform (CnC) developed by St. John's Episcopal Church in Oakland, California (Forward Movement, 2012)—Twenty lessons of classroom work, field trips, mentor relationships, and challenges to take responsibility for understanding faith and its power. Youth discover their own voice as they confirm their beliefs. For middle school youth.

Confirm not Conform for Adults developed by St. John's Episcopal Church in Oakland, California (Forward Movement, 2012)—Based on the youth curriculum, CnC for Adults focuses on the spiritual and developmental needs of people in the middle of their life. The lesson plans cover the basics on Bible, creeds, prayer books, and sacraments, topics that may have been ignored or lost in the mists of time. Participants experiment with different spiritual practices to find what ones work best for them. For adults.

The Discovery Series: A Christian Journey developed by the Episcopal Diocese of Texas (Forward Movement)—A DVD series (five video programs, sixteen segments) that includes a brief history of the Episcopal Church, an instructed Eucharist, spiritual gifts assessment, the Bible, Jesus, the Creeds, and Baptism. Each course has two to four video segments (approximately fifteen minutes each) to be followed by group work (about forty-five minutes). Also available in Spanish. For older youth and adults.

The Episcopal Handbook (Morehouse Publishing, 2008)—A fun, accessible companion handbook for anyone who wants a quick and humorous breakdown of truths about the Episcopal Church alongside the basics of Christianity. It includes a concise glossary of Episcopal terms, maps, diagrams, and illustrations in one little volume. For youth and adults.

Episcopal Questions, Episcopal Answers: Exploring Christian Faith by Ian S. Markham and C. K. Robertson (Morehouse Publishing, 2014)—A question/answer format of what one might ask about the Episcopal Church with quick, easy, and non-threatening responses on the most central and compelling elements of the faith.

I Believe (LeaderResources)—A two-year program to experience and reflect on what it means to name Jesus Christ as Lord and Savior in the context of the Episcopal Church based on biblical stories. Includes classroom reflection, retreats, community service, mentors, prayer, worship, and internships in the congregation. For youth.

I Will, With God's Help by Mary Lee Wile (Morehouse Education Resources, 2000)—A six- to twelve-week confirmation program based on the Baptismal Covenant that can be adapted for retreats, with readings from the Gospel of Luke (Mentor Guide by Linda

Nichols also includes the gospels of Mark, Luke, and John for each year of the Lectionary). Components include a Leader's Guide, Youth Journal, Adult Journal, and Mentor Guide. For youth and adults.

Jesus Was an Episcopalian (and You Can Be One Too!): A Newcomer's Guide to the Episcopal Church by Chris Yaw (LeaderResources, 2008)—A provocative book that spurs conversation about the Episcopal Church of the past as well as the future, including service to the world through such vehicles as the Millennium Development Goals. Also available in Spanish. For adults.

Living Water: Baptism as a Way of Life by Klara Tammany (Church Publishing, 2002)— Eight group sessions focus repeatedly on water, first as a natural element necessary to life, then as a symbolic element necessary to spirituality. Gradually, through prayer, song, scripture, silence, poetry, visual arts, storytelling, group discussion, and personal reflection, water—as baptismal element—gains importance while exploring the Baptismal Covenant. Includes group and individual discussion and study options. For high school and adults.

My Faith, My Life: A Teen's Guide to the Episcopal Church by Jenifer Gamber (Morehouse Publishing, 2006, with a revised edition to be published Fall 2014)—Written for teens as they explore the Episcopal Church and prepare for the rite of Confirmation. Chapters include: The Bible, Baptism, Church History, Prayer, Worship, the Episcopal Church. Leader's Guide available separately. For youth.

People of the Way: Renewing Episcopal Identity by Dwight J. Zscheile (Morehouse Publishing, 2012)—Draws on multiple streams of Anglican thought and practice to craft a vision for mission that addresses the Episcopal Church today, built upon the past while looking at today as a new Apostolic Era. Questions for discussion at the end of each chapter. For adults.

Sealed and Sent Forth developed by the Episcopal Diocese of East Carolina (Leader-Resources)—Fifteen two-hour sessions that are formatted to include worship, content, discussion, reflection, and community building. It examines what it means to be a Christian and an Episcopalian, and invites participants to examine what a particular Christian community does and means. For older youth and adults.

The Seekers developed by Rick Brewer and OACES (LeaderResources)—A two-year program (twenty-five sessions each year) of lesson plans with background, activities, and retreats with the purpose to call young people into adulthood by discovery, wonder, and reflection on life in light of our Christian tradition. Four units cover faith, life, self, and values. For young adults.

Those Episkopols by Dennis R. Maynard (Dionysus Publications, 2007)—Offers eleven short chapters on topics that an inquirer to the Episcopal Church might ask, such as: Can you get saved in the Episcopal Church? Why do Episcopalians read their prayers? Why do Episcopalians reject biblical fundamentalism? For adults.

Unabashedly Episcopalian: Proclaiming the Good News of the Episcopal Church by Andrew Doyle (Morehouse Publishing, 2012)—Mines the Baptismal Covenant while sharing the unique gifts and stories of the Episcopal Church, encouraging the reader to witness to their faith in their neighborhoods and out in the world. Online discussion guide available. For adults.

Welcome to Anglican Spiritual Traditions by Vicki K. Black (Morehouse Publishing, 2010)—Explores the different ways that Christians, particularly Anglicans, have prayed, thought about, and lived out their faith through the centuries. Six chapters focus on the promises we make at baptism and how they inform and shape our relationships, decisions, and actions. Discussion questions for each chapter. For adults.

Welcome to the Episcopal Church: An Introduction to Its History, Faith, and Worship by Christopher L. Webber (Morehouse Publishing, 2009)—One of several in the "Welcome to" series, this volume offers the history, worship, beliefs, spiritual life, organization of the Church, mission and outreach, and the reading of Scripture from an Episcopal perspective. Discussion questions accompany each of the seven chapters. For adults.

What Episcopalians Believe: An Introduction by Samuel Wells (Morehouse Publishing, 2011)—An introduction to Episcopal identity as part of Anglicanism in four parts: The Faith (God, Jesus, Israel, Holy Spirit, creation, kingdom, salvation), Sources of the Faith (Scripture, tradition, reason), The Order of the Faith (worship, ministry, mission), and The Character of the Faith (English legacies, American dreams, global dimensions). Study guide included. For adults.

Your Faith, Your Life: An Invitation to the Episcopal Church by Jenifer Gamber with Bill Lewellis (Morehouse Publishing, 2009)—In conversational style, the language of worship, theology, church structure, and sacraments are unpacked offering a framework to exploring the meaning and practices of the Episcopal Church and faith through the lens of: "Be Attentive. Be Intelligent. Be Reasonable. Be Responsible. Be in Love." Questions for discussion at the end of each chapter. For adults.

Sample Diocesan Guidelines

Episcopal Diocese of Connecticut [1]
Guidelines for Confirmation, Reception & Reaffirmation

1. Candidates for Confirmation should be in 10th grade, 16 years or older
2. Preparation should be a minimum of one academic year (September–May) with a preference for two years of preparation prior to the rite of Confirmation with opportunities for ongoing formation and education for all ages post-Confirmation
3. The Faith Community should take an active role in supporting confirmands through prayer, recognition, and serving as mentors to journey with each candidate
4. Clergy and Laypersons share leadership in the preparation of candidates for Confirmation, Reception, and Reaffirmation
5. The Deanery is a source of support and companionship in preparing confirmands through retreats, mission opportunities, and the Rite of Confirmation service
6. The bishop is an integral part in the preparation of confirmands
7. Components for preparation should include:

   - Scripture
   - The Book of Common Prayer
   - Service & the Life of the Baptized
   - Mission & Community
   - Prayer
   - Faith & Practice—to include participation in worship, stewardship, Christian ethics, moral decision making, and theological reflection
   - Episcopal polity

Diocese of Western Massachusetts [2]
Guidelines for Confirmation Preparation

Preparation needs to include at least the following:

1. Minimum of 16 hours of Catechumenal preparation
2. Move toward young people not being confirmed until at least 10th grade
3. Daily prayer and weekly Sunday Eucharist
4. Regular reflection on Scripture
5. Small group faith sharing and prayer
6. Content should include: introduction to the Bible and history of the Church, BCP, Catechism, Baptismal Covenant, and Stewardship (gifts, time & money)

---

1. *http://www.ctdiocese.org/images/customer-files/2005CTConfirmationGuidelines.pdf*
2. *http://www.diocesewma.org/wp-content/uploads/2013/04/REV-3.2013GUIDELINES-FOR-CONFIRMATION-PREPARATION.pdf*

7. Practice "proclaiming by word and deed the Good News of God in Christ" (i.e., training, action, and reflection in witness (evangelism) and service (justice & peace)

Episcopal Diocese of Alabama [3]
Anglican Essentials: A Course of Adult Catechesis in the Diocese of Alabama

A 128-page resource for teaching inquirers about the Episcopal Church offers a format of hospitality and community building, with a curriculum that has been written following this outline for group study and discussion.

1. Church History: An Introduction

    a. English Heritage
    b. The American Church

2. Anglican Worship and the Book of Common Prayer, Liturgy and Piety
3. Sacramental Life

    a. Baptism and The Holy Eucharist
    b. Other Sacramental Rites

4. The Authority of Scripture

    a. The Bible's Place in Anglican Theology
    b. The Bible's Authority from Five Perspectives

5. Christian Life and Faith

    a. The Nicene Creed
    b. Baptismal Covenant
    c. Ministers of the Church
    d. The Structure and Polity of the Church
    e. Moral Decision Making
    f. Engaging the World

6. The Anglican Spirit

Episcopal Diocese of Maryland [4]
Guidelines for Confirmation

Confirmation services are an integral and important part of our diocesan life together. The individuals you present bring an exciting energy, faith, and love to our Church. The service gathers family and friends from all generations to witness an individual's mature, adult

---

3. A nine-month curriculum for seventh, eighth, and ninth graders has also been written and can be found at: *http://s3.amazonaws.com/dfc_attachments/public/documents/100359/Final_Final_curriculum_2_06_blwhite_doa.pdf; adult material: http://s3.amazonaws.com/dfc_attachments/public/documents/100106/final_curriculum_pdf_format_billie.pdf*

4. Full guidelines can be accessed at: *http://www.ang-md.org/christian_formation/forms/2009-confirmation.pdf*

commitment to their faith and to the promises made for them at baptism. The ceremony and presence of the bishop accentuate the gifts and importance of our Episcopal tradition and faith. It is in that spirit that your bishops have established diocesan standards for confirmation and offer support and resources for your confirmation programs. Confirmations and Receptions may be done as part of the regular bishops' visitations, on special feast days, and in regional and diocesan gatherings. The bishops will also schedule diocesan confirmation during the Great Fifty Days of Easter.

It is important to emphasize here that Confirmation is an individual adult rite of discipleship. To that end, to receive the sacramental rite of Confirmation in the Diocese of Maryland, it is expected that each candidate will have received quality instruction in the parish, and that each person presented:

- will have attended one of four Bishops' Teaching Days.
- should be old enough to make a mature decision. The minimum recommended age is fifteen, but pastoral exceptions are possible.
- is a regular participant in the life, worship, education, and outreach of the congregation presenting them.
- will gather to meet with the bishop one hour before the service.

The Episcopal Diocese of Massachusetts[5]
Theological, Ecclesial, Missiological, and Practical Assumptions

1. Confirmation (including Reception) is the occasion for a mature affirmation of faith, and opportunity for a person to claim for oneself the promises made for him or her at Baptism (or reaffirm promises made earlier) in the context and presence of:

    - The local faith community (parish) that nurtures faith and sends forth disciples to serve the risen Christ
    - The wider faith community (diocese/deanery) that is a broad and diverse sign of the one, holy, catholic, and apostolic church which joins God's mission in the world through partnerships and collaborative ministries
    - The bishop as apostle, theological, visionary leader for mission, and pastor

2. Confirmation stresses the mission part of Baptism and looks ahead to a life of witness and service. It reflects a personal sense of calling to glorify God, letting Christ's light shine.
3. Confirmation is a continuation of lifelong formation, a semi-colon, not a period.
4. Confirmation represents the continuing work of the Holy Spirit in a person's life and faith community (parish and diocese).
5. Confirmation is about the transformation of individuals, communities of faith, and God's church. It entails openness to change, risk, and faith.
6. Confirmation strengthens, commissions, and sends forth candidates and faith communities to join God's mission of reconciling love in the world. The great Commandment and Great Commission are at the heart of our understanding of Confirmation.

---

5. *http://www.diomass.org/webfm_send/1665*

Episcopal Diocese of Virginia [6]
Guidelines for the Rites of Initiation

Those who were baptized as infants and who for the first time wish as mature adults to commit themselves to Christ and to renew their Baptismal Vows will receive the episcopal laying on of hands for confirmation.

Those persons who have been baptized as adults in the Episcopal Church and who later wish to renew their baptismal vows before the congregation will be presented, not for confirmation, but for reaffirmation.

In recent time, it has been customary to present young people for confirmation at an age that has been used historically to mark the division between childhood and the taking on of the increasing responsibilities of adulthood. But our culture no longer recognizes so clear a line of division and instead allows young people to enter into an extended period of "no-longer-a-child/not-yet-an-adult," during which we see young people at different paces becoming clearer on who they are and what they want their values to be. It seems desirable to consider the end of this period in young people's lives, rather than the onset of it, as the appropriate time to offer the opportunity of making the commitment to faith represented by confirmation.

It is, therefore, important to wait until an age when the individual may clearly express his or her own desire to affirm faith. It is during the years from twelve to sixteen that individuals work out their identity and it is to be hoped that their life in the community of the church during that time will have prepared them to decide to assume mature responsibility for their faith. It is also at sixteen that young adults are encouraged to take their responsibility in government of the church by voting for vestry members (Canon 11, Section 3).

Individuals do work out their identity at different paces and different ages, however, and in this culture, the beginning of this identity crisis is earlier than twelve years of age. No guidelines will be set by the Diocese of Virginia for fixing an age for confirmation, but clergy, catechists, and parents are urged to consider the rationale of confirmation being normative for those of high school years or older. The entire Christian community needs to be made aware of their responsibility to lead each young person to make an individual and mature decision to present himself/herself to the bishop for confirmation as directed by the Book of Common Prayer, page 412.

The primary intent of confirmation is to provide one the occasion in the presence of the bishop and the gathered community, to profess Jesus Christ as Lord and Saviour and to invoke God's help through the Holy Spirit to live as a witnessing Christian in the world.

Episcopal Diocese of Newark [7]
Guidelines for Confirmation Preparation

The following guidelines are to assist our congregations and all who bear the responsibility of helping our youth make a "mature commitment" to the Christian faith in our Episcopal tradition in preparing candidates for Confirmation.

6. http://www.thediocese.net/Customer-Content/WWW/CMS/files/Rites_of_Initiation.pdf

7. http://www.dioceseofnewark.org/sites/default/files/resources/ConfirmationPolicy.pdf

1. Candidates for Confirmation must be in the 8th grade or older.
2. Preparation should be a minimum of one academic year of 40 hours with a preference for two years of preparation which would include opportunities for ongoing formation as suggested below.
3. The congregation should take an active role in supporting confirmands through prayer, recognition, and mentoring.
4. The Rite of Confirmation is held after Easter at Trinity and St. Peter's Cathedral by district. Some districts may decide to combine their confirmations. The Confirmation for District 10 is held at St. Paul's Church in Paterson.

Required Activities:

- Attendance at all confirmation classes with a specified number of excused absences.
- Mission/Outreach: making your faith real by answering Christ's command to love one another (ex: 8 hours of service or 3 projects).
- Worship: mandatory attendance at specified services, especially Principal Feasts and Holy Days.
- Community-Based Education: have regular faith conversations with parents/guardians/mentors; have some homework assignments that are completed together with parents/guardians/mentors; have the vestry and confirmands share a meal.

Recommended Activity: Diocesan Confirmation Retreat
   Content:

- Bible
- Book of Common Prayer
- Sacraments

- Christian Identity
- Prayer
- Ministry

The bishop should be assured that those presented for Confirmation have demonstrated a personal understanding of the Christian faith, have been instructed in Christian doctrine and discipline, and are able to make a personal confession of their faith. It is expected, too, that candidates for Confirmation will be prepared to undertake a disciplined ministry in the mission of the Church.

Episcopal Diocese of Albany [8]
Confirmation Requirements

Minimum Requirements

To be confirmed in the Episcopal Diocese of Albany, you must meet the following requirements.

- Must be a baptized Christian
- Must be at least 13 years old

---

8. *http://www.albanyepiscopaldiocese.org/ConfirmationGuide2009.pdf*

- Must write a letter to the bishop (see below)
- The Episcopal Diocese of Albany Confirmation Curriculum is highly recommended as the curriculum used to teach our young people. If a Rector/Vicar chooses not to use this curriculum then he or she will need to review with the bishop the method of preparation and how the foundations of our faith were carried out with the confirmands.

Suggested Requirements

Every parish has different circumstances, so therefore we have a list of suggested requirements for each parish to add if they wish.

- Sponsors/mentors
- Community service
- Serve on the altar
- Learning about a ministry of our parish

Letter to the Bishop

The purpose of the letter to the bishop is to help the bishop get to know the confirmands before his arrival at the service. The letter also provides a way for the confirmands to show they have thought through their faith, and are able in their own words to explain their faith and why they want to be confirmed. The letters do not need to be long and they do not need to be typed, but confirmands need to write about these things:

1. Write a little about your faith journey and about your faith in Jesus Christ as your savior.
2. Write about a mission trip you have taken or a ministry at our church in which you have been involved and why it has been meaningful to your life of faith.
3. Write about your ongoing call to be a member of the Body of Christ—what new ministry will you do in your church, or what ongoing ministry will you continue?